THE HEART OF WHITENESS

CONFRONTING RACE, RACISM,
AND
WHITE PRIVILE

D1013513

BY ROBERT JENSEN

CITY LIGHTS
SAN FRANCISCO

CITY LIGHTS PUBLISHERS · 1955 · 2005 ·

Cover design by Yolanda Montijo
Typography by Harvest Graphics
Book design by Elaine Katzenberger

Library of Congress Cataloging-in-Publication Data

Jensen, Robert, 1958-
   The heart of whiteness : confronting race, racism, and white
privilege / by Robert Jensen.
         v.   cm.
   Contents: Introduction : hating myself to save myself—Race words
and race stories—Facing the truth : past, present, and future—The
emotions of white supremacy   I : fear and guilt—Dodges and
diversions—The emotions of white supremacy   II : anger—Against
diversity, for politics—Conclusion : white people's burden.
   ISBN-10: 0-87286-449-9
   ISBN-13: 978-0-87286-449-8
   1. United States—Race relations.   2. Whites—Race identity—
United States.   3. Whites—United States—Social conditions.
4. Whites—United States—Psychology.   5. Jensen, Robert, 1958-
6. Jensen, Robert, 1958—-Relations with African Americans.
7. Whites—United States—Biography.   8. Men, White—United
States—Biography   I. Title.
   E184.A1J425 2005
   305.8'00973—dc22

                                                    2005007522

Visit our website: www.citylights.com

City Lights books are edited by Lawrence Ferlinghetti and Nancy J.
Peters and published at the City Lights Bookstore, 261 Columbus
Avenue, San Francisco, CA 94133.

This book is dedicated to Dave,

whose last name—to my shame—

I never bothered to learn.

"The conquest of the earth, which mostly means the taking it away from those who have a different complexion or slightly flatter noses than ourselves, is not a pretty thing when you look into it too much."

Joseph Conrad, *Heart of Darkness*, 1902

"What one begs the American people to do, for all our sakes, is simply to accept our history."

James Baldwin, "The American Dream and the American Negro," 1965

ACKNOWLEDGMENTS

MANY PEOPLE HAVE influenced my thinking about race and politics, including activists and writers I have never met, as well as my friends, colleagues, and allies. Special thanks to Jim Koplin, for demonstrating that it's possible to live honestly as a white person with integrity; and to Bernestine Singley, for both her ferocity and generosity in helping a white boy find his way. There can be joy in our present struggles, and hope for the future, when one struggles alongside such people.

My thanks also to Elaine Katzenberger, Stacey Lewis, and Chanté Mouton from City Lights for, once again, making the process of imagining, writing, editing, publishing, and selling a book so pleasurable.

CONTENTS

THE HEART OF
WHITENESS

INTRODUCTION
Just a Joke

I AM WHITE. MY most immediate ancestors come out of Scandinavia and northern Europe. My skin is pale. I am a Caucasian. I was born and raised in the very white state of North Dakota. I'm as white as white gets in the United States of America. I am a white-bred, white-bread white boy.

My life has been lived white in a white-supremacist society. As I was growing up in North Dakota, that fact was invisible to me. Once aware of it, I spent a number of years trying to avoid dealing honestly with that fact. Over the years I've spent a lot of energy dodging certain truths and trying to cover up my failures, from myself and from others. All that effort has left me tired; avoiding obvious truths takes a lot of energy.

So, in this book, I'm going to try something different: I'm going to be as honest as I can. I'm going to try to tell as many truths as I can face, as bluntly as I can. I am going to write as harshly as I can, in part out of exhaustion—I'm too tired to struggle with being polite. But the harshness also comes out of love. Dorothy Day of the Catholic Worker Movement was fond of quoting a line from Dostoevsky's *The Brothers Karamazov:*

"Love in action is a harsh and dreadful thing compared with love in dreams."

It is good to dream, to love in dreams, to dream of a day beyond white supremacy. But those dreams will remain only dreams unless we speak and act, harshly. We need that kind of love—not just tough love, but a truly harsh and dreadful love.

But, all that said, let's ease into this. Let's start at an easy place. Let's look at a joke. Just a joke, but one that can help us learn something about what it means to be white in this world.

The Joke

A white friend and I are taking a walk. Somewhat nervously, he tells me that he wants my opinion on a joke he told to an all-white group at a recent business dinner, a joke that had made some people at the table uncomfortable. "I want to know," he says, "whether you think the joke is racist."

At that moment, I hate the world we live in. I hate the conversation that I know he and I are about to have. I hate the fact that I can't escape it.

Before he even tells me the joke, the answer is obvious: Of course the joke is racist. He understands that because he knows enough to form the question. Though he is struggling to understand why, his gut tells him it is a racist joke. At some level he knows that he told a racist joke to a group of white people. Why is he asking me? Is it in the hope that I'll tell him it wasn't so bad after all? Or does he need someone to confirm what he knows in his gut and tell him that he is still a good person?

Here's the joke: "Why did they have to cancel the Miss Ebonics pageant? Because no one wanted to be Miss I-da-*ho*."

My reply to him: It's not only racist, it's misogynist. It is a joke at the expense of black people and women. It's a sick and ugly joke. He asks me why.

At this point, I want to strangle him for forcing me into this role. I want to tell him, "It's racist and sexist, and if you gave it five seconds of thought, you could explain why, and you have no right to make me do it for you." But, of course, he has every right to ask me. I should be glad he asked me; he is taking a chance by opening a discussion around a difficult issue. My reaction is less about anger at him as it is about fear of myself. I'm angry at him, but I am afraid of myself.

Here's my answer:

Part I: Any invocation of Ebonics for humor by white people is almost certainly going to be racist. It's based on an implicit definition of Ebonics—"black vernacular" or "African American vernacular English"—as less-than, as a defective form of so-called Standard English. Whatever one thinks about the issue of how to handle Ebonics in schools, the discussion of whether or not it is a "real" language system is possible only in a racist culture. The routine white denigration of this particular language system reveals an opinion not about the words being spoken but about the people speaking them. Ebonics, like any other human language, is systematic and rule-governed. It is a way of speaking, fundamentally regular and expressive, like all others. The fact that people like to make fun of it—the fact that it can be the basis for jokes—is an indication of the enduring white-supremacist character of the United States.

Part II: Any use of "whore" or its derivatives is a symbolic assault on women who are prostituted, those who can be bought and sold for the pleasure of men, one of the most vulnerable groups of women. The use of "ho" by a white person in this context typically is not only sexist but racist as well, because it plays on the notion that black men are somehow more misogynist than men from the dominant white culture. It dumps onto black men the sexism of white men, a kind of cleansing projection that leaves white men feeling better without having to challenge ourselves.

My friend makes a half-hearted attempt to defend himself. He understands the ugly politics of the joke, he says, but still appreciates the clever word play. If you set aside the politics, it is funny, he contends.

Part III: Jokes are funny only in context. There is no such thing as abstract clever word play. Words have meaning in the world in which we live, not in the abstract. Take away the politics, and there is no joke. The joke wouldn't make any sense. If the joke is funny, it's funny precisely because it's racist and sexist.

My conclusion to him: There is no place to hide. You told a racist and sexist joke, and you're accountable for it. Deal with it. I ask him whether he would have told the joke if there had been a black person in the group. He acknowledges that he likely would not have. Maybe that's a clue something is wrong, I suggest.

Nothing about this is fun, for either of us. The exchange is tense. Eventually it becomes clear that I have made my points and that pursuing it further would benefit no one. I know my friend will take the critique seriously and not brush off the issue. He'll think about it, honestly. So will I. He's a decent person who is serious about issues of justice. Our friendship continues to this day, valued by both of us.

Still, at that moment, I hate him. And I hate myself. Why? Because even though I know that at this point in my life I wouldn't tell a joke like that, I understand why it's funny. I didn't find that particular joke funny, but I know what it feels like to hear a joke based on the denigration of black vernacular and to laugh, even if I laugh only inside my own head. I've trained myself not to laugh out loud. But I know why it's funny, and I know why it's racist to find it funny, even if I mute my laughter. When my friend told me that joke, I had to face that fact about myself, which was much harder than facing him.

So, I hate myself, which is appropriate.

When I express these kinds of thoughts and feelings, I am routinely told that I have to get beyond hatred. I have to love myself. I disagree. Hate is the first word I grab to describe the feeling. Maybe it isn't exactly the right word, but I use it because it conveys the intensity that I think is appropriate. Maybe I should think of it as another kind of love, just a love particularly harsh and dreadful. Maybe there is no word that can convey what I feel. If hate isn't it, I know that platitudes about love don't capture what I feel. Why should I love such ugly flaws and failings? I agree that love matters in this world, but I don't think white people should love their whiteness. Better for everyone, I think, that we take a shot first at hating it.

I don't mean white people should hate themselves for having pale skin, for something we were born with. I think we white people should sometimes hate ourselves for what we do, or don't do, in the world, for the choices we make about that white skin. In other words, we should hate whiteness and be accountable for our own complicity with whiteness. We live in a white-supremacist society and benefit from white privilege. We should hate that fact, and if we haven't done enough to change that world, well . . .

And that's the rub: Whatever we have done, it's not enough. It's not enough because the white-supremacist society still exists. The fact that it still exists should cause us discomfort, every day.

Does that seem too strong? Too harsh? Too dreadful? Actually, I think this kind of hating ourselves and our privilege is the first step toward being able to truly love. Poet Nikki Giovanni made this point to writer James Baldwin, about the relationship of black to white:

> Giovanni: I think one of the nicest things we created as a generation was just the fact that we could say, Hey, I don't like white people.
> Baldwin: It's a great liberation.
> Giovanni: It was the beginning, of course, of being able to like them.[1]

The same holds for the relationship of white to ourselves. When we can acknowledge that we don't—or shouldn't—like some aspects of ourselves, it can be the liberation that ends with a more authentic loving of ourselves and others.

Saving Ourselves

I am a white person living in a white-supremacist society. I am surrounded by, enveloped in, trapped by—I am forced to live in—a depraved and degraded whiteness. I want to escape this trap. I want to live in a world in which I can at least imagine that someday I will be able to stop being white. I want to be able to dream of being a human being instead of a white person. That's

---

[1] James Baldwin and Nikki Giovanni, *A Dialogue* (Philadelphia: J. B. Lippincott Co., 1973), p. 28.

where this book starts, with an acknowledgment that this writing is born of selfishness. I want to find a way out of whiteness so that I can claim my own humanity. This book is about the traps and my escape route. If that seems self-indulgent, it is.

In any struggle to end a system of oppression, those on the bottom of the hierarchy have an obvious motivation to resist the system: to remove from their lives the source of the oppression. But what of those who in some way benefit from the oppression? What of those of us on top of the hierarchy? In the arena of race, what about us white people? What might motivate us to act for social change?

There is always an argument from justice, the simple plea for decent human lives for everyone. If we see someone being hurt, we know we should help. When we see someone being brutalized, we know it is wrong. When these things happen systemically, it is just as obvious that we should act, though it typically is more difficult to know for sure what actions can change the system. Resisting oppressive systems that cause injuries and deprive others of their rights is the appropriate thing to do if one takes seriously the ethical or religious principles by which most of us claim to live. But however powerful that argument from justice, we can observe that it does not always motivate people with unearned privilege to work to change the system that gave them the privilege. We can observe that privileged people's commitment to social change tends to be stronger and more reliable when it is grounded in an acknowledgment of their own interests.

So, in addition to arguments from justice we also should pursue arguments from self-interest. In the arena of racial justice in the contemporary United States, this means articulating the painful truth that whiteness is depraved and degraded. To accept whiteness, to truly believe in it, is to deform oneself. The privileges and material benefits that come from being white in a white-supremacist society come at a cost to us white people. Whiteness is based on lies not only about others but lies about ourselves, and we can't lay claim to our full humanity until we find our way out of the web of denial.

If we think of self-interest only in a narrow material sense, it may not be clear why white people should want to contribute to changing that system. But if we ask what might be in the interest of our best selves,[2] the picture changes. If we expand the definition of self-interest beyond the short term and material, we can come to terms with what both my friend and I knew as we talked about the joke: Somewhere down in our guts we understand that in an oppressive system such as white supremacy, the unearned privileges with which we live are based on the suffering of others. We know that we have things because others don't. We may not want to give voice to that feeling, but it is impossible to ignore completely. And it doesn't feel good, in part because to be fully human is to seek communion with others, not separation from them, and one cannot find that connection under conditions in which unjust power brings unearned privilege. To be fully human is to reject a system that conditions your pleasure on someone else's pain.

I believe we all want to be fully human. In this book I want to talk about the lies—and about the system they support—that not only deny the humanity of non-white people but also keep me from my own.

---

[2] This idea is developed in John Stoltenberg, *The End of Manhood: A Book for Men of Conscience* (New York: Dutton, 1993).

RACE WORDS AND RACE STORIES

IN ANY POLITICAL discussion it's important to define terms precisely and use them honestly. Much of the discussion about the terminology of race has focused on the words used to describe non-white groups — Indian versus Native American, black versus African American, Hispanic versus Latino, and so on. Those discussions are important, but they are not subjects on which the opinion of a white guy is needed. In this chapter I want to focus on a different set of terms and the politics that underlie them.

People of color?

I typically use the term "non-white" instead of the more common "people of color." At first glance, that may seem odd given that "people of color" is, especially in liberal circles, the most common term one hears for people in the United States who are not white. It's also a common term used by people of color to describe themselves when they are not speaking of specific racial and ethnic groups. Of course all these language choices have a politics — Negro does not carry the same meaning as black or African American, for example. Terms and their meanings change over time. As in virtually all issues about naming, the assumption should be that people have a right to choose how others refer to them, at the personal and the collective levels.

But what of terms that do not describe specific racial or ethnic groups but all groups that are not white? For many years, "minorities" was the most common term and is still often used, reflecting the reality that white people are (for the time being, but not for long) the majority in the United States. "People of color" seems to have replaced that as the preferred term. My argument against using it may seem counterintuitive at first: The problem with "people of color" is that it takes the focus off white people. In a book that critiques white supremacy, that may seem a strange complaint. Shouldn't we be trying to take the focus off white people, who dominate society and can so easily drown out the voices of non-white people? Of course we should; we white people need to realize we are not the point of reference for everything. White is not, by definition, the norm, the standard, the best. White is just white.

But politically, white is not just white, of course. White is power. And using the terms white/non-white reminds us of that. What do people of color have in common? That is, what makes the category "people of color" make sense? The only commonality is that the people in that category are on the subordinated side of white supremacy. Nothing intrinsically links people of indigenous, African, Latino, and Asian descent in the United States except their common experience of being targeted, abused, and victimized—albeit in different ways at different times—by a white-supremacist society. Take that experience away, and the category of "people of color" vanishes. The people, of course, don't vanish, nor does their color change. But nothing links them except the experience of oppression. And the group perpetrating that oppression is white, another socially created category defined by power.

So, I want to put "white" at the center, but not in the sense of valorizing it or claiming it as a norm. Just the opposite. I want to frame the issue as white and non-white to highlight the depravity of white supremacy and identify it as the target. In this sense, I think "white/non-white" more clearly marks the political nature of the struggle, whereas "people of color" for many tends to shift the focus from white supremacy to the varied cultures of those non-white people. Again, in many situations that shift is important, as white people learn more about other cultures and, we hope, understand both the unique contributions that various cultures make and the way in which all cultures share certain common qualities and values. Such understanding can contribute to the breakdown of white supremacy.

But a cultural focus can easily overwhelm the political when white people do not want to confront white supremacy and white privilege. So, I am constantly looking for ways to highlight those realities: The problem is the depravity of white, the unjust exercise of power in a white-supremacist society, the unearned privileges that come with whiteness. I want to put the focus on white to press forward the project of destroying white power.

White supremacy

The United States of America at the beginning of the twenty-first century—a century and a half after the end of slavery, four decades after the passage of the Civil Rights Act—is a white-supremacist society.

By "white supremacist," I mean a society whose founding is based in an ideology of the inherent superiority of white

3

Europeans over non-whites, an ideology that was used to justify the crimes against indigenous people and Africans that created the nation. That ideology also has justified legal and extralegal exploitation of every non-white immigrant group, and is used to this day to rationalize the racialized disparities in the distribution of wealth and well-being in this society. It is a society in which white people occupy most of the top positions in powerful institutions, with similar privileges available in limited ways to non-white people who fit themselves into white society.

That claim will strike many as ludicrous. Yes, we may have some remnants of racial inequality, and of course there are lingering racial tensions, and it's true that there are still some white people who hold openly racist beliefs. But white supremacist? The entire society? How can one make such a claim?

It's easy. We can start with the numbers. President Bill Clinton promised us a national conversation on race in the 1990s. The conversation didn't get very far, but his Council of Economic Advisors for the President's Initiative on Race did gather a large amount of data.[3] They detailed how, on average, whites are more likely than members of racial/ethnic minorities to:

• Attend primary and secondary schools with smaller class sizes.

• Have access to computer technology in public schools and at home during primary and secondary schooling.

• Attend and graduate from a four-year college or university.

• Earn higher salaries.

---

[3] Council of Economic Advisors, "Changing America: Indicators of Social and Economic Well-Being by Race and Hispanic Origin," September 1998. http://w3.access.gpo.gov/eop/ca/index.html.

- Retain employment during a downturn in the economy.
- Be covered by health insurance and consequently gain access to health care.
- Survive certain life-threatening illnesses.
- Experience more favorable housing conditions (less crowding, less crime, less litter and deterioration, and fewer problems with public services).
- Spend a smaller percentage of household income on housing.
- Have unimpeded access to home mortgage loans and home ownership.
- Own stocks, mutual funds, and IRA accounts.
- Gain a substantial net worth.

If we look just at the statistics about blacks and whites, the numbers are stark. According to a 2004 study by United for a Fair Economy, on some measures black Americans had fallen behind white Americans in recent decades:[4]

- The typical black family had 60 percent as much income as a white family in 1968, but only 58 percent as much in 2002.
- One in nine African Americans cannot find a job. Black unemployment is more than twice the white rate, a wider gap than in 1972.
- Black infants are almost two and a half times as likely as white infants to die before age one, a greater gap than in 1970.
- White households had an average net worth of $468,200 in 2001, more than six times the $75,700 of black households. In

---

[4] United for a Fair Economy, "The State of the Dream 2004: Enduring Disparities in Black and White," January 2004. http://www.faireconomy.org/press/2004/StateoftheDream2004.pdf.

1989 (the oldest comparable data available), average white wealth was five and a half times that of black wealth.

On many measures, closing the gap between black and white is decades, or centuries, away:

• At the slow rate that the black-white poverty gap has been narrowing since 1968, it would take 150 years, until 2152, to close.

• For every dollar of white per-capita income, African Americans had fifty-five cents in 1968 and only fifty-seven cents in 2001. At this pace, it would take blacks 581 years to get the remaining forty-three cents.

• Although white home-ownership has jumped from 65 percent to 75 percent since 1970, black home-ownership has only risen from 42 percent to 48 percent. At this rate, it would take 1,664 years to close the gap, about fifty-five generations.

• If current rates of incarceration continue, one out of three African-American males born today will be imprisoned at some point during their lifetimes.

• At the current pace, blacks and whites will reach high school graduation parity in 2013, six decades after the *Brown v. Board of Education* school desegregation decision. And college graduation parity wouldn't be reached until 2075, more than 200 years after the end of slavery.

What does white supremacy mean in day-to-day life? In the United States, a black applicant with no criminal record is less likely to receive a callback from a potential employer than a white applicant with a felony conviction.[5] In other words, being

---

5 Devah Pager, "The Mark of a Criminal Record." *American Journal of Sociology,* 108:5 (March 2003): 937–975.

black is more of a liability in finding a job than being a convicted criminal. Studies show that from the mid-1990s through the beginning of the new century, such discrimination in low-wage jobs has remained constant. These statistics led the researcher to conclude that even if employers are not consciously discriminating against black applicants, "there are a lot of unconscious processes that come into play that bias or distort employers' perceptions of the quality or suitability of minority applicants."[6]

But numbers can never tell the whole story. The statistics have to be made real through the experiences and stories of people who live with the consequences of white supremacy. Such testimony of non-white people is readily available to anyone who wants to take the time to listen or read. If you aren't sure where to start, try something simple: Pick up a book or go online. Are you interested in the history and reality behind those statistics about black America? Try an anthology of important African-American writing, such as *Let Nobody Turn Us Around: Voices of Resistance, Reform, and Renewal.*[7] Or just type "driving while black" into an Internet search engine and read a few of the stories.

White Privilege

In a white-supremacist society, white people will have privilege. That's hardly a radical claim, yet it continues to be contro-

---

[6] Interview with Devah Pager, November 20, 2003. http://www.north-western.edu/observer/issues/2003-11-20/newsfeed.html.

[7] Manning Marable and Leith Mullings, eds., *Let Nobody Turn Us Around: Voices of Resistance, Reform, and Renewal* (Lanham, Md.: Rowman and Littlefield, 2000).

versial in many sectors of U.S. society. In 1986, Peggy McIntosh presented a paper that pointed out that although many white people were willing to acknowledge that racism put others at a disadvantage, they were less forthright about how that same system gives whites advantages of various kinds. Widely anthologized and republished,[8] the essay prompted discussion of white privilege in some circles, but such a simple assertion sparks considerable resistance from many white people.

White privilege, like any social phenomenon, is complex. In a white-supremacist society, however, all white people have some sort of privilege in some settings. There are general patterns, but such privilege plays out differently depending on context and other aspects of one's identity. So, it's true that a non-white manager can have power over a white employee who is in a subordinate position, and that a non-white person living in the upper-middle class enjoys a higher standard of living than a working-class white person. Class affects people's lives. It's also true that in this society men have power over women, and that power can cross racial lines. Gender affects people's lives.

But none of that derails a simple observation: In this white-supremacist society, whiteness consistently conveys certain privileges. A simple illustration of this was broadcast on the ABC News program "Primetime."[9] Using a hidden camera, the producers conducted a standard experiment to determine whether a white and black man would be treated differently in the world.

---

[8] Margaret L. Anderson and Patricia Hill Collins, eds. *Race, Class and Gender: An Anthology,* 5th ed. (Belmont, Calif.: Wadsworth, 2004); Michael S. Kimmel and Abby L. Ferber, eds., *Privilege: A Reader* (Boulder, Colo.: Westview, 2003).

[9] "True Colors," aired September 26, 1991.

Two men who worked for the Leadership Council for Metropolitan Open Communities in Chicago (a nonprofit group that works to ensure equal opportunity in housing) temporarily relocated to St. Louis, where they looked for an apartment, hunted for a job, shopped for shoes and cars, and went about the day-to-day business of living. The two men were alike in most every respect—age, education, background, work history—except race. In some situations, the men were treated equally. But a pattern of disparate treatment emerged, captured on video:

• The black man was ignored by salespeople in stores or tailed as a possible shoplifter, while the white man was greeted warmly and allowed to browse without suspicion.

• When both pretended to have locked their keys in their cars, the white man was showered with offers of help by passersby while the black man was ignored.

• At a used car lot, the white man was quoted more favorable terms for purchasing the same car.

• The white man was shown an apartment at a complex where the black man was told there were no vacancies.

• While the black man walked down the street in a predominantly white part of town, a white man leaned out of a passing car and said "Little far south, ain't it?" to let him know that he was in the wrong part of town.

All of that is evidence of white privilege. The anecdotal evidence of the program is backed up by statistics. But the real core of white privilege is revealed in the reaction of many white people to such a claim. When I showed the program to a class at the University of Texas, for example, a white student said, "The program isn't balanced. It shows the black guy getting harassed in a white neighborhood, but what would happen to me if I went to a black neighborhood?" Well, what would happen? Maybe a white man walking in a predominantly black part of town late at night would be at greater risk of being robbed or attacked than if he were black. Maybe. But even if that were the case, there are a few important differences. In most cases, white people can decide whether or not they want to go into a predominantly black neighborhood. In most cases, black people have no choice but to deal with a predominantly white world. If they want to get a job or secure a bank loan or buy a car, they will have to deal routinely with white people in a white world. The program we had just finished watching had detailed all the places where the black man had faced varying levels of discrimination or hostility. It was a difficult program to watch; the black man in the segment described the pain he felt, even though he knew it was "just a test." Yet instead of dealing with that, this white student in class had immediately raced to the one example he could think of—feeling unsafe walking in a black neighborhood—to begin the discussion. Or, more accurately, to try to end the discussion. That's part of white privilege—the privilege to ignore the reality of a white-supremacist society when it makes us uncomfortable, to rationalize why it's not really so bad, to deny one's own role in it. It is the privilege of remaining ignorant because that ignorance is protected.

There's one other disturbing aspect of that program, which I didn't notice until I had watched it several times. The show ends with one final illustration of discrimination: The two men go out on a New York street to catch a cab, with the black man standing in the foreground and the white man farther down the street. Both have their arms outstretched to hail a cab. Diane Sawyer, the reporter for this segment, points out that the first cab that pulls over glides past the black man and stops for the white man. The message is clear: In virtually every aspect of life—from the risk of racist violence, to getting a job, to finding a place to live, to the simple act of hailing a cab—the black person will face struggles and threats that the white person will not.

Cut back to the studio. Sawyer is at the desk, smiling happily. "We're going to motor on off ourselves," she says.

Such is television news; everything has to end on an upbeat note. But there was something incredibly depraved about the ending. After such a painful segment in which the white supremacy of the society was revealed, how could she smile? Even if such inanity is part of the script, how could she smile? How could she talk about "motoring off," making a bad joke that played on what we had just seen? Yes, I know, that's how television news operates. They smile, even when they have just finished reporting on a tragedy. But isn't there something sick about a white person delivering an indictment of white supremacy and then smiling? That's white privilege, too.

Yes, there really is white privilege and it really matters

The claim that white people are privileged in a white-supremacist society doesn't seem controversial on the surface. But lots of white people, in my experience, contest it, including many who do not consider themselves to be racist. Some simply claim that the United States has moved past racism and is not a white-supremacist society, though it's unclear how they would explain the racialized disparities. Others claim that in recent years white privilege has eroded and been replaced by reverse racism against whites. Others simply see such privilege as inevitable. Here are the common reactions I get when I write or speak on the subject, and my typical responses:

1. White privilege doesn't exist anymore because affirmative action has made being white a disadvantage.

It is certainly true that the use of affirmative action programs means that there are times when a white person does not get a job or slot in a university because a non-white person is chosen to fill that position. Whites often complain that the affirmative action, therefore, deprives them of things to which they are entitled. But that begs the obvious question: Do white people benefit from a much more extensive kind of affirmative action provided by white privilege? How do the expectations that whites come to have about what they "deserve" affect their perception of what they are "losing"? Does an extremely limited attempt to combat racism such as affirmative action erase that much larger system of white privilege? Do such limited programs erase the white privilege built over 500 years that pervades our society?

2. White privilege exists, but it can't be changed because it is natural for any group to favor its own.

Any assertion about "natural" human behavior should be approached skeptically. This argument tries to make what is a human choice appear to be outside of human control, which is a dodge to avoid moral and political responsibility for the injustice we continue to live with. It's true that history is littered with conflicts of various kinds between peoples. But if the creation of the rigid racial categories on which contemporary white supremacy is based were "natural," why haven't all peoples organized the world that way throughout time? And, even if it were natural in some sense, does that mean we simply accept it?

3. White privilege exists, but people have unearned privileges of all kinds. For example, tall people have unearned privilege in basketball,

*but we don't ask tall people to stop playing basketball nor do we
eliminate their advantage in the game. So, don't worry about it.*

The obvious difference is that racial categories are invented;
they carry privilege or disadvantage only because people with
power create and maintain the privilege for themselves at the
expense of others. The privilege is rooted in violence and is
maintained through that violence as well as more subtle means.
Such is not the case with advantages in basketball. I can't change
the world so that everyone is the same height, so that everyone
has the same shot at being a pro basketball player. In fact, I
wouldn't want to; it would be a drab and boring world if we
could erase individual differences like that. But I can work with
others to change the world to erase the effects of differences such
as race that have been created by one group to keep others down.

*4. White privilege exists, and that's generally been a good thing because
white Europeans have civilized the world, even if along the way some
bad things may have happened.*

These people often argue the curiously contradictory position that (1) non-whites and their cultures are not inferior, but
(2) white/European culture is superior. My experience suggests
many white people actually believe this, though they are hesitant to articulate it in public. It is, of course, an irrational position, but it's not surprising that people who are raised on the
notion that certain kinds of art, writing, music, political institutions, and moral ideas are the pinnacle of human creativity
might be hesitant to give that up. As for the civilizing effect of
Europe, we might consider five centuries of brutal colonialism
and World Wars I and II, and then ask what "civilized" means.

The first step for whites is simple: to acknowledge that we are
white people living in a white-supremacist society. We can

struggle to shed a white-supremacist ideology. We can join with non-white people in struggles for racial justice. But we cannot give away our white privilege. We can be attentive to situations in which white privilege is clearly benefiting us and disadvantaging others, and try to intervene to stop it. But we cannot pretend to live in a world in which we do not benefit from white privilege, until white supremacy is no longer a defining feature of our society. The only question is: What will we white people do with our privilege?

Race

Race is a fiction we must never accept.

Race is a fact we must never forget.

Both those statements are true. Race, as a biological concept, is a fiction. Although recent work on the human genome reveals some biological patterns that correlate with one's ancestors' continent of origin, there are not distinct races as people typically think of them. There is one human race, and the people who are part of it have various kinds of physical differences. The belief that what we have come to call "races" are meaningful biological categories has been discredited. The American Anthropological Association's statement on race articulates this clearly:

> In the United States both scholars and the general public have been conditioned to viewing human races as natural and separate divisions within the human species based on visible physical differences. With the vast expansion of scientific knowledge in this century, however, it has become clear that human populations are not unambiguous, clearly demarcated, biologically distinct groups. Evidence from the analysis of genetics (e.g., DNA) indicates that most physical variation, about 94 per-

cent, lies *within* so-called racial groups. Conventional geographic "racial" groupings differ from one another only in about 6 percent of their genes. This means that there is greater variation within "racial" groups than between them.[10]

But in a social sense, of course, race is very real. Although it is likely true that humans have always used some method to mark inclusion in, and exclusion from, a social group, it is not true—as many people assume—that humans have always marked race in the way that developed in modern European society. There is nothing natural or inherent about racial categorizing. Quoting from the anthropologists again:

> The "racial" worldview was invented to assign some groups to perpetual low status, while others were permitted access to privilege, power, and wealth. The tragedy in the United States has been that the policies and practices stemming from this worldview succeeded all too well in constructing unequal populations among Europeans, Native Americans, and peoples of African descent. Given what we know about the capacity of normal humans to achieve and function within any culture, we conclude that present-day inequalities between so-called "racial" groups are not consequences of their biological inheritance but products of historical and contemporary social, economic, educational, and political circumstances.[11]

So, we are left with the conclusion that race is not natural but created. It is a socially and historically constructed concept. "Race"

---

[10] American Anthropological Association, Statement on "Race," May 17, 1998. http://www.aaanet.org/stmts/racepp.htm.

[11] Ibid.

means whatever people decide it means. And the people with the most to say about what it means tend to be the people in positions of power in political, economic, and ideological institutions — which, in the United States today, continue to be white people.

Racism

Racism is typically distinguished from mere prejudice in terms of power. Prejudice — negative or hostile attitudes toward members of a group based on some shared trait, perceived or real — becomes racism when one group has the power to systematically deprive the members of another group of rights and privileges that should come with citizenship and/or being a human being. The International Convention on the Elimination of All Forms of Racial Discrimination defines "racial discrimination" as

> any distinction, exclusion, restriction or preference based on race, color, descent, or national or ethnic origin which has the purpose or effect of nullifying or impairing the recognition, enjoyment or exercise, on an equal footing, of human rights and fundamental freedoms in the political, economic, social, cultural or any other field of public life.[12]

Though the United States has been a white-supremacist country for its entire history, ideas about race are not completely static. Howard Winant describes "processes of racial signification," the way in which race is given meaning, as "variable, con-

---

[12] International Convention on the Elimination of All Forms of Racial Discrimination, Part I, Article I, adopted and opened for signature and ratification December 21, 1965, and entry into force January 4, 1969. http://www.unhchr.ch/html/menu3/b/d_icerd.htm.

flictual, and contested at every level of society."[13] Non-white people have always, and one can assume will always, resist racist attempts to define and constrain them. Some whites will ally themselves with those struggles, while others will try to block them. Various forces in society are pursuing "racial projects," which Winant defines as "simultaneously an interpretation, representation, or explanation of racial dynamics and an effort to organize and distribute resources along particular racial lines."

Using these terms, we're all in the race game, so to speak, either consciously or unconsciously. We can overtly support white-supremacist racial projects. We can reject white supremacy and support racial projects aimed at a democratic distribution of power and a just distribution of resources. Or we can claim to not be interested in race, in which case we almost certainly will end up tacitly supporting white supremacy by virtue of our unwillingness to confront it. In a society in which white supremacy has structured every aspect of our world, there can be no claim to neutrality.

Institutionalized racism

As Winant points out, processes of racial signification go on at all levels, "from the intrapsychic to the supranational." That means we have to decide what kind of racial projects to pursue at all levels, from our own attitudes and behaviors in day-to-day life to the structure of our economic, political, and cultural life. It's relatively easy for white people to focus on the struggle to change racist behaviors and attitudes at the personal level but

---

13 Howard Winant, *Racial Conditions* (Minneapolis: University of Minnesota Press, 1994), p. 24.

ignore questions at more systemic levels. But, of course, changing oneself in a society that remains unchanged can be only part of a progressive racial project.

In this context, people often speak of fighting institutionalized racism, indicating a desire to take on the problem at the systemic level. When people use the concept, I often ask them what they mean by it. The common answer is that racism can continue in a society or organization, even if individuals aren't overtly racist, because of the structure or procedures that an institution uses. But when asked to identify those structures and procedures, and explain how they replicate racism, people often stumble. I find that institutionalized racism is a term that is often used without a clear sense of its meaning. How does racism become institutionalized? Two examples might help to illustrate.

Example 1: It is widely accepted that education is crucial to democracy and a just society. If there is no equality in education, there is no equality in society, especially as information-based specialized training becomes more crucial for making a decent living. The fact that wealthy people can afford expensive private schools and private tutoring for their children already calls into question the society's real commitment to equality in education. Given that those able to afford such enhanced educational opportunities are disproportionately white raises uncomfortable questions. But I'll put those issues to the side here and concentrate only on the public school system.

In the United States, education funding typically is tied in part to local property taxes. Wealthier school districts can raise more money for education than poorer districts. Wealth correlates with race. And the United States is still overwhelmingly segregated in terms of housing. Put those facts together, and you have one predictable result: Non-white children will, on average when compared with white children, attend schools with fewer financial resources.[14] That means those students will go to schools with less experienced teachers, fewer technological resources, fewer and older textbooks, fewer and less well-funded enrichment programs, and school facilities not kept up as well. That is to say, those non-white children will not have access to, on average, an education equal to white children. That is to say, education is not equal from the standpoint of resource allocation. Before one even gets to questions of how white teachers and administrators sometimes build cultural and/or linguistic chauvinism into curriculum and classroom practices, we can see that the system is structured in ways that disadvantage many non-white students.[15]

In the past, unequal schools were the result of planning, of official policies of de jure segregation; white people deliberately created such a system. But today, this state of affairs is more complex. Public education is not racist because each day a bunch of overtly racist white people come to work and deliberately try to maintain a racist school system. It is the product of many decisions over many years, some of them no doubt made by people of conscience who thought of themselves as anti-racist, but who maintain an institutional structure that creates

---

14 For an example of how this has played out in one school district, in Milwaukee, see Michael Barndt and Joel McNally, "The Return to Separate and Unequal," *Rethinking Schools*, Spring 2001. http://www.rethinkingschools.org/archive/15_03/Sep153.shtml.

15 Thanks to my University of Texas colleague Angela Valenzuela for her help with these ideas.

conditions that support white supremacy. If people in the United States were truly interested in racial justice, the funding mechanisms for public schools would be drastically altered and a system devised that equalized funding. Such steps wouldn't fix the problem, but it would be a start. Such steps not only have not been taken in the United States but have never been seriously considered.

Example 2: On most U.S. university campuses with a Greek system, fraternities and sororities are segregated.[16] Any Greek organization that enforced such segregation by official policy — a "whites-only" rule — would be bounced off campus. But the continued existence of overwhelmingly segregated fraternities and sororities on many campuses, as a result of traditions and practices that are not overtly racialized, runs afoul of no regulations. But two crucial questions arise.

First, how does the presence of virtually all-white Greek organizations affect the racial climate on campus? It's reasonable to assume that on a campus where official segregation was abandoned only a few decades ago and non-white students still routinely report they do not feel particularly welcomed on campus, the presence of high-visibility and prestigious groups that remain exclusively or largely whites-only adds to the sense of the university as a white-supremacist institution. Also, the persis-

---

[16] For accounts of how this plays out in similar fashion in different regions of the country, see Patrik Jonsson, "South wrestles with segregated sororities: At University of Alabama, Greek system remains divided along racial lines, despite prodding by faculty," *Christian Science Monitor*, September 18, 2001. http://www.csmonitor.com/2001/0918/p4s1-ussc.html; and Eirik Ott, "Race divides Greek system," *The Orion* (California State University–Chico), May 5, 1998. http://orion.csuchico.edu/Pages/vol40issue14/d.15.html.

tence of overtly racist parties at white Greek houses—such as "ghetto parties" in which attendees mock urban blacks, or fake slave auctions—adds to the sense of a campus as a white space.[17] The existence of predominantly non-white Greek organizations, especially black fraternities and sororities, does not change this reality. When unwelcome and/or made to feel uncomfortable in white organizations, it's hardly surprising that non-white students would form their own groups.

Second, Greek organizations are more than just clubs for students while on campus. They create social networks that endure beyond college days and provide entrée into business and politics. One study found that a quarter of chief executives at the 500 largest corporations in the United States were fraternity members and that "once they've graduated, [members] can tap into the network of past fraternity brothers or sisters who litter all tiers of corporate America." The conclusion:

> A mere 8.5 percent of full-time university undergraduates are members of either a fraternity or a sorority. Not only have fraternities been the breeding ground of those 120 Forbes 500 chief executive officers, they also have spawned 48 percent of all U.S. presidents, 42 percent of U.S. senators, 30 percent of U.S. congressmen, and 40 percent of U.S. Supreme Court justices, according to data from The North-American Interfraternity Conference.[18]

The vast majority of these people are, of course, white.

---

[17] See, for example, Bryce Nieman, "Racism troubles Big 12 schools," *Oklahoma Daily*/U-WIRE, January 29, 2002.

[18] David Dukcevich, "Best fraternities for future CEOs," Forbes.com, January 31, 2003. http://www.forbes.com/2003/01/31/cx_dd_0131 frat.html.

So, the continued existence of a segregated Greek system perpetuates white supremacy, not necessarily because those who support the system have an overt white-supremacist ideology or intend the organizations to have that function. But in a white-supremacist society, the failure to intervene to change the course of the institution means that the institution will perpetuate white supremacy. Racism is no longer official policy of the institution, but its practices are racist. If a university with a Greek system that has this character were serious about creating a truly nonracist university, one easy way to begin the process would be to eliminate the Greek system or enact policies that make desegregation mandatory within a limited time frame. In most universities, either policy is unthinkable.

The stories we tell

We use terms to label ourselves and others. We struggle over what the terms mean and how they should be applied. But we also define ourselves by the stories we tell. There are two different stories I could tell about myself. Which is true?

Story #1

I was born in a small city in North Dakota, to parents in the lower middle class who eventually scratched their way to a comfortable middle-class life through hard work. I never went hungry and always had a roof over my head, but I was expected to work, and I did. From the time I started shoveling snow as a kid, to part-time and summer jobs, through my professional career, I worked hard. From the time I was old enough to hold a steady job, I have held one. I was a conscientious student who studied hard and took school seriously. I went to college and did fairly well, taking a year off in the middle to work full-time. After graduation I worked as a journalist, in nonglamorous jobs for modest wages, working hard to learn a craft. I went on to get a master's degree and returned to work before eventually pursuing a doctorate so I could teach at the university level. I got a job at a major university and worked hard to get tenure. I'm still there today, still working hard.

Story #2

I was born in a small city in North Dakota, to white parents in the lower middle class who eventually scratched their way to a comfortable middle class life through hard work. The city I grew up in was almost all white. It was white because the indigenous population that once lived there was either exterminated or pushed onto reservations. It was extremely cold in the winter there, which was okay, people would joke, because it "kept the riff-raff out." It was understood that riff-raff meant people who weren't willing to work hard, or non-white people. The assumption was there was considerable overlap in the two groups.

I was educated in a well-funded and virtually all-white school system, where I was taught a variety of skills, including how to take standardized tests written by and for white people. In those schools my accomplishments were applauded and could be seen as part of a long line of accomplishments of people who looked like me. I mostly studied the history of people who look like me. Indigenous people were mostly a footnote.

I worked in part-time and summer jobs for which I was hired by other white people. One of those jobs was in a warehouse owned by a white man with whom my father did business. In that warehouse, we sometimes hired day labor to help us unload trucks. One of the adult men we hired was Indian. His name was

Dave. We called him "Indian Dave." I, along with other white teenage boys working there, called him Indian Dave. We didn't give it a second thought.

I went to college in mostly white institutions. I had mostly white professors. I graduated and got jobs. In every job I have ever had, I was interviewed by a white person. Every boss I have ever had (until my current supervisor, who was hired three years ago) has been white. I was hired for my current teaching position at the predominantly white University of Texas, which had a white president, in a college headed by a white dean, and in a department with a white chairman that at the time had one non-white tenured professor.

I have made many mistakes in my life. But to the best of my knowledge, when I have screwed up in my school or work life, no one has ever suggested that my failures were in any way connected to my being white.

True Stories

Both of those stories are true. The question is, can we recognize the truth in both of them? Can we accept that many white people have worked hard to accomplish things, and that those people's accomplishments were made possible in part because they were white in a white-supremacist society? Like almost everyone, I have overcome certain hardships in my life. I have worked hard to get where I am, and I work hard to stay there. But to feel good about myself and my work, I do not have to believe that "merit" alone, as defined by white people in a white-supremacist country, got me here. I can acknowledge that in addition to all that hard work, I got a significant boost from white privilege, which continues to protect me every day of my life from certain hardships.

At one time in my life, I would not have been able to say that, because I needed to believe that my success in life was due solely to my individual talent and effort. I saw myself as the heroic American, the rugged individualist. I was so deeply seduced by the culture's mythology that I couldn't see the fear that was binding me to those myths, the fear that maybe I didn't really deserve my success, that maybe luck and privilege had more to do with it than brains and hard work. I was afraid I wasn't heroic or rugged, that I wasn't special.

I let go of some of that fear when I realized that, indeed, I wasn't special, but that I was still me. What I do well, I still can take pride in, even when I know that the rules under which I work are stacked in my benefit. Until we let go of the fiction that people have complete control over their fate—that we can will ourselves to be anything we choose—then we should expect to live with that fear. Yes, we should all dream big and pursue our dreams and not let anyone or anything stop us. But we all are the product both of what we will ourselves to be and what the society in which we live encourages and allows us to be. We should struggle against the constraints that people and institutions sometimes put on us, but those constraints are real, they are often racialized, and they have real effects on people.

So, are all white people racist?

If "racist" means the expression of overtly racist ideologies about the inherent inferiority of non-white people and support for practices that would reflect that belief, then it seems clear that most white people in the United States are not racist. The Ku Klux Klan and other overtly white-supremacist groups exist, but they are considered fringe by most people. Yet at the same time, virtually all white people have to face the fact that racism lurks in our hearts and minds as a result of being raised in a white-supremacist society; it is difficult—maybe impossible—to find a white person who hasn't been affected in some way by such a society. But the question "are all white people racist?" misses the point. Better to ask: "Do most white people recognize that they live in a white-supremacist society that nominally supports ideals of racial justice but continues to accept practices and institutions that maintain white privilege?" From there, we can ask: "Do most white people engage in critical self-reflection about white privilege or undertake political projects to challenge institutionalized racism?"

There is wide agreement in the contemporary United States that racism is an ugly phenomenon. There also is, understandably, a desire on the part of many to put the struggle over that racism to rest—to acknowledge that it is a part of our history, acknowledge that it lingers on today, but suggest that it is increasingly less relevant in our society. Today's debates about racial justice usually focus on the contemporary claims, on the assumption that there is wide agreement about the racism in our past. That's a crucial error, for this country has never come to terms with that racist past, which suggests that is a place to start.

FACING THE TRUTH: PAST, PRESENT, AND FUTURE

P EOPLE TEND TO be selective about how they use history. When people want to invoke some grand and glorious aspect of the past, then history is all-important. We are told how crucial it is for people to know history, and there is much hand-wringing about the current generation's lack of knowledge about, and respect for, that history. In the United States, we hear constantly about the wisdom of the founding fathers, the spirit of the early explorers, the determination of those who "settled" the country, the heroism of soldiers—and about how crucial it is for everyone to learn about these things.

But when one brings to a discussion of history those facts that contest the celebratory story and make people uncomfortable—such as the deeply racist history of the United States—there are two common responses. One is, "Well, yes, but you have to judge people by the standards of their time, not ours." More on that at the end of this chapter.

The other attempt to divert people from the truth is the accusatory question, "Why do you insist on dwelling on the past?" Ironically, the same people who extol the virtues of knowing history and highlight the importance of that knowledge for contemporary citizenship now suddenly argue that we shouldn't spend too much time thinking about history, or at least some aspects of history. It appears that those parts of our history that prop up our sense of ourselves as a noble and righteous people are the proper focus of study and public comment; what's important to know is what can be celebrated to make ourselves feel good. Those who also want to include in that discussion the uglier aspects of our past are accused of looking to cause trouble, of undermining our children's faith in their country. One person who disliked my discussion of such unpleasant facts once suggested I was "trying to humble our proud nation."

So, let me be clear: I do want to undermine people's faith in this country, especially young people's. More humility and less pride would be a good thing. I do not mean I want to undermine a faith in the ideals of democracy and freedom, or a faith in the capacity of ordinary people to take charge of their own lives and live those ideals. Instead, I want to undermine the intellectually lazy and morally bankrupt practice of rewriting history to exclude or downplay inconvenient facts so that in the present we can pretend that the United States is the ultimate fulfillment of history, the paragon of virtue, the repository of justice. That faith is a fool's faith, and it can only exist in a country in which history is not a subject for honest examination but an ideological tool to support the existing distribution of power (which, sadly, history too often is in too many societies). I believe in the relevance of the past to understanding ourselves in the present. I believe in history, and I love the study of it. But I believe in honest history, which includes the failures as well as the triumphs of a people. Such a history inevitably will undermine one's faith in the United States, which is the first step toward a better United States.

Three racist holocausts

Here's where that discussion of history must start: The United States has perpetrated three holocausts[19] in its history, and all three were justified and/or made possible by racism. Those holocausts created the United States, propelled the United States into the industrial era, and created a worldwide U.S. empire—and in the process killed millions around the world, impoverished the lives of millions more, and ravaged other cultures.

Here's where that discussion of history leads: Conventional accounts of U.S. history tend to treat racism as a stain on an otherwise healthy—some would say divinely inspired—society. The United States, according to this mythology, was born out of a desire for freedom and would become both the model of, and vehicle for, freedom around the world. The treatment of non-white peoples was an aberration that would come to be fixed in time, as white people understood their non-white brothers and sisters to be deserving of that same freedom. It can be difficult for white Americans to recognize that white supremacy is the rot at the core of the project and always has been. The country's

---

[19] I am aware of the debate over whether the term "holocaust" should be reserved for the Nazi's attempted extermination of Jews in Europe in the World War II era. Millions of people—Jews, Roma, Slavs, Communists, homosexuals, and other official enemies of the Nazi regime—died in an incredibly intense outburst of criminality and cruelty. In the examples I discuss here, millions also died as a result of decisions of officials, backed by a significant portion of the dominant population. To honor the memory of all these victims, and to try to prevent such events in the future, I think the term "holocaust" should be applied to all situations of such magnitude.

formation, economic expansion, and imperial endeavors are inextricably intertwined with racism. White society's version of U.S. history is weighed down by narcissistic fantasies of innocence, entangled in a self-serving web of stories of nobility. Those denials of the past are crucial to those who cannot honestly confront the present.

Let's start with the first racist holocaust that began when Europeans landed in the region that was eventually to include the United States. There were people here when Columbus landed, of course. Population estimates vary widely, but a conservative estimate is 12 million north of the Rio Grande, perhaps 2 million in what is now Canada and the rest in what is now the continental United States. By the end of the so-called Indian Wars, the 1900 census recorded 237,000 indigenous people in the United States. That's an extermination rate of 95 to 99 percent. That is to say, the original European colonists and their heirs successfully eliminated almost the entire indigenous population.[20] Said differently: The entire land base of the new nation was secured by a genocidal campaign that was almost completely successful. Almost every Indian died in the course of the European invasion to create the United States. Millions of people died for the crime of being inconveniently located on land the Europeans desired.

But were those indigenous peoples really people in the eyes of the invaders? Were they full human beings? Many Europeans were not so sure. George Washington, the father of our country,

---

[20] See Ward Churchill, *A Little Matter of Genocide* (San Francisco: City Lights Books, 1997) for a review of the data and a compelling argument.

in 1783 said he preferred buying Indians' land rather than driving them off it because that was like driving "wild beasts" from the forest. He compared Indians to wolves, "both being beasts of prey, tho' they differ in shape."[21] But, of course, it would turn out that Washington's "benevolent" attitude toward Native peoples and his beliefs on how best to remove them from their land did not carry the day. But his categorization of them as sub-human would remain the prevailing opinion as the land was cleared by more brutal methods. Thomas Jefferson — author of the Declaration of Independence, which refers to Indians as the "merciless Indian Savages"— also was known to romanticize Indians and their culture. But in 1807 Jefferson wrote to Secretary of War Henry Dearborn, instructing him to prepare for war and to let the Indians understand the danger they faced. "We too are preparing for war against those, and those only who shall seek it; and that if ever we are constrained to lift the hatchet against any tribe, we will never lay it down till that tribe is exterminated, or driven beyond the Mississippi." The drafter of one of our foundational documents of liberty was clear: "In war, they will kill some of us; we shall destroy all of them."[22]

As the genocide was winding down, President Theodore Roosevelt defended the expansion of whites across the continent as an inevitable process "due solely to the power of the mighty civilized races which have not lost the fighting instinct, and which by their expansion are gradually bringing peace into the

---

[21] George Washington, letter to James Duane, September 7, 1783. http://teachingamericanhistory.org/library/index.asp?document=359.

[22] Richard Drinnon, *Facing West: The Metaphysics of Indian-hating and Empire-building* (Norman: University of Oklahoma Press, 1997), p. 96.

red wastes where the barbarian peoples of the world hold sway."[23] Roosevelt, whose face is carved into Mount Rushmore as testament to his wise and brave leadership, once said, "I don't go so far as to think that the only good Indians are dead Indians, but I believe nine out of ten are, and I shouldn't like to inquire too closely into the case of the tenth."[24]

But wait, many will say, whatever the racism of some U.S. leaders, this claim of genocide ignores the fact that many of the indigenous people died as a result of disease. But the fact that a large number of indigenous people died of disease doesn't absolve white people. Sometimes those diseases were spread intentionally, and even when that wasn't the case the white invaders did nothing to curtail contact with Indians to limit the destruction. Some saw the large-scale death of indigenous people as evidence of the righteousness of their mission; God was clearing the land so that civilized whites could take their rightful place upon it. Whether the Indians died in war or from disease, starvation, and exposure, white society remained culpable.[25]

So, the establishment of the United States killed millions of indigenous people. One will find some mention of this in U.S. history textbooks, though rarely will the term "genocide" be used or the bitter racism of U.S. "heroes" be acknowledged. The fate of indigenous people is impossible to ignore completely in conventional history, but the inability of the culture to come to

---

[23] Theodore Roosevelt, *The Strenuous Life* (New York: The Century Co., 1901), p. 38.

[24] David E. Stannard, *American Holocaust: Columbus and the Conquest of the New World* (New York: Oxford University Press, 1992), p. 245.

[25] Again, this argument is made most clearly by Churchill, *A Little Matter of Genocide.*

terms with the depravity of the crime is instructive in trying to understand the nature of racism in the United States. Some of our most revered political leaders planned, executed, and celebrated a genocide that secured the land base of the country. These men often justified the genocide by asserting that the non-white people being murdered were not fully human, or at least had "no rights which the white man was bound to respect."[26] Which takes us to the next story.

The second American holocaust was African slavery, another subject that American history textbooks can't ignore but rarely deal with as a holocaust. Again, the number of non-white people murdered is in the millions. There is no way to know exactly how many Africans died during the process of enslavement in Africa, the Middle Passage, and in the New World. But it is safe to say that tens of millions of people were rounded up and that as many as half of them died in the process. This holocaust was instrumental in the emergence of the United States as an industrial power. Historians and economists continue to debate how central slavery was to U.S. economic development, but it's clear that slave-grown cotton provided crucial export earnings that aided U.S. economic expansion and spurred industrial development in the North.[27]

Although slavery was first justified on the basis that Africans were not Christian and therefore not civilized, that rationale

---

[26] The infamous phrase comes from *Dred Scott v. Sandford*, the 1856 U.S. Supreme Court case that declared no slave or descendant of a slave could be a U.S. citizen.

[27] For a review, see Joe R. Feagin, *Racist America: Roots, Current Realities, and Future Reparations* (New York: Routledge, 2000), Chapter 2, "Slavery Unwilling to Die."

became harder to defend as some blacks converted to Christianity, learned English, and adopted European ways. The justification shifted to a biological argument; blacks were not simply culturally inferior but biologically inferior in intellectual and moral terms, and hence inherently incapable of self-government. This was the so-called "scientific" racism that bolstered an argument for permanent enslavement.[28]

So, the land base and industrial development of the country are bound up in two holocausts that killed millions, both backed by a racist ideology that used superficial human differences to justify exploitation that employed barbaric methods. Several things are striking about how the nation deals with this history. First, it wasn't until the social and political ferment of the 1960s that something approaching an honest account of the scale of these crimes could be discussed. Second, even after those cultural and intellectual changes opened up the discussion, significant segments of society still can't face the fact that these crimes were in facts crimes—committed intentionally by people who had the capacity to know they were crimes—let alone face what these crimes mean for us today.[29] Third, and for me most important, is how contemporary discussion of these subjects—including by people who understand the impact of this history—is so dispassionate, so lacking in outrage. The

---

[28] See George M. Fredrickson, *Racism: A Short History* (Princeton, N.J.: Princeton University Press, 2002).

[29] If one doubts that claim, think of the hysteria that pours out every second Monday in October on Columbus Day when critics point out Columbus's role in the first holocaust. See Ward Churchill, "Deconstructing the Columbus Myth." http://www.transformcolumbusday.org/columbus_myth.htm.

near-extermination and enslavement of peoples is rarely engaged by the dominant society. The depth of the horror is never fully acknowledged.

That third racist holocaust perpetrated by the United States—the attack on the Third World to extend and solidify the U.S. empire—goes on as I write. Most chart the beginning of the external U.S. empire-building phase with the 1898 Spanish-American War and the conquest of the Philippines that continued for some years after. That project went forward in the early twentieth century, most notably in Central America, where regular U.S. military incursions made countries safe for investment.[30] But the empire emerged in full force after World War II, as the United States assumed the role of the dominant power in the world and intensified the project of subordinating the developing world to the U.S. system.[31] Those efforts went forward under the banner of "anticommunism" until the early 1990s, but continued after the demise of the Soviet Union under various other guises, most notably the so-called "war on terrorism." Whether it was Latin America, southern Africa, the Middle East, or Southeast Asia, the central goal of U.S. foreign policy has

---

[30] A particularly blunt assessment comes from a participant in the project, Marine Major General Smedley Butler, who in retirement condemned U.S. policy in "War Is a Racket." http://www.veteransforpeace.org/war_is_a_racket_033103.htm.

[31] For a comprehensive list, see "That 'Most Peace-Loving of Nations': A Record of U.S. Military Actions at Home and Abroad, 1776–2003," in Ward Churchill, *On the Justice of Roosting Chickens: Reflections on the Consequences of U.S. Imperial Arrogance and Criminality* (Oakland, Calif.: AK Press, 2003), pp. 39–85; and Zoltan Grossman, "From Wounded Knee to Afghanistan." http://www.zmag.org/list2.htm.

been amazingly consistent: to make sure that an independent course of development did not succeed anywhere. The "virus" of independent development could not be allowed to take root in any country out of a fear that it might infect the rest of the developing world.[32]

To call this a racist holocaust is controversial in a country in which the propaganda system describes these Third World endeavors of the United States as exercises in the liberation of other people. But, again, the victims—the vast majority of them non-white—can be counted in the millions. In the Western Hemisphere, U.S. policy was carried out mostly through proxy armies, such as the Contras in Nicaragua in the 1980s, or support for dictatorships and military regimes that brutally repressed their own people, such as El Salvador. The result throughout the region was hundreds of thousands of dead—millions across Latin America over the course of the twentieth century—and whole countries ruined.[33]

Direct U.S. military intervention was another tool of U.S. policymakers, with the most grotesque example being the attack on Southeast Asia. After supporting the failed French effort to recolonize Vietnam after World War II, the United States invaded South Vietnam and also intervened in Laos and Cambodia, at a cost of 3 to 4 million Southeast Asians dead and a region destabilized. To prevent the spread of the "virus" there, we dropped 6.5 million tons of bombs and 400,000 tons of napalm on the people of Southeast Asia. Saturation bombing of

---

[32] Noam Chomsky, *World Orders, Old and New* (New York: Columbia University Press, 1996).

[33] Eduardo Galeano, *Open Veins of Latin America*, rev. ed. (New York: Monthly Review Press, 1997).

civilian areas, counterterrorism programs and political assassination, routine killings of civilians, and 11.2 million gallons of Agent Orange to destroy crops and ground cover—all were part of the U.S. terror war.[34] Decades after the war ended, people continued to die from unexploded ordnance left from the war, especially the diabolically cruel cluster bombs.

These wars, interventions, and covert operations were motivated by a desire for power and resources, not racism. But in a white-supremacist society, it's easier to justify an assault on another country when the people of that country are not white, in part because of the sense of cultural superiority ("These people need our help to figure out how to live") and in part because of whites' devaluation of the lives of non-white people (seen in Americans' description of Vietnamese as "gooks"[35]). In one of the most outrageous expressions, General William Westmoreland, the U.S. commander during the Vietnam War, explained: "Well, the Oriental doesn't put the same high price on life as does the Westerner. Life is plentiful, life is cheap, and, as the philosophy of the Orient expresses it, life is not important."[36] As the United

---

[34] Jonathan Neale, *A People's History of the Vietnam War* (New York: New Press, 2003); Marilyn B. Young, *The Vietnam Wars, 1945–1990* (New York: HarperCollins, 1991).

[35] Such terms continue to be used, though usually not in polite company. However, Arizona senator John McCain, considered a moderate Republican, only stopped using the term during his 2000 presidential campaign when reporters and staff members begged him to drop such an openly racist term from his vocabulary. See Jeff Cohen, "Covering McCain: Are Journalists On the Bus or Off the Bus?" Fairness and Accuracy in Reporting, February 24, 2000. http://www.fair.org/articles/mccain-bus.html.

[36] "Hearts and Minds," 1974, Peter Davis, dir.

States showed its high regard for human life by destroying a society, U.S. leaders could opine about how those uncivilized Asians just didn't value life as we do.

This imperial racism is complex, interwoven with a pathological patriotism and ethnocentrism. There has been, for example, anti-Arab racism in black and Latino as well as white communities during the U.S. invasions of Arab countries. This racism/ethnocentrism was portrayed in the film *Three Kings*,[37] set during the 1991 Gulf War. In one scene a white solider uses the term "dune coon" to refer to an Iraqi. A black soldier objects to that term and "sand nigger," another derogatory term for Arabs, because they draw on longstanding white racist terms for blacks in the United States. The white solider defends himself by saying that even their captain uses such terms. Another white solider responds: "That's not the point, Conrad. The point is that Towel Head and Camel Jockey are perfectly good substitutes." The black soldier's response: "Exactly!" The scene is played for laughs, but it reflects a reality that is deadly serious. Racist slurs are acceptable, but the right people must be targeted at the right time, all part of a racist project to dehumanize the victims of the country's aggression.

U.S. history is many things. It is the story of brave pioneers from Europe willing to strike out in unknown territory to build a new life. It also is the story of barbaric racist bloodbaths. It is the story of hard work. It is the story of murder and theft. Welcome to the world, in which heroes often have less heroic sides as well, including some of the heroes who are at the center of the country's founding mythology.

---

[37] *Three Kings*, 1999, David O. Russell, dir.

The standards of the time

Let's return to this often-heard claim that we can't judge people of another era by the standards of our time. This is often asserted when one looks back in U.S. history to evaluate the actions of our founding fathers, for example. When one critiques people such as Thomas Jefferson, not only for owning slaves but for expressing ugly racist beliefs, the response is that he was simply expressing an idea prevalent in the world in which he lived, as if there was no way to think outside of racism. This approach avoids a simple question: "Were there any people expressing alternative ideas at the time?"

Of course there were. Among them was Thomas Paine, another major figure in the establishment of the United States who is widely known for his best-selling 1776 pamphlet *Common Sense*, which made the case for independence from England. What is less well known about Paine is that he was an opponent of slavery. He arrived in America in 1774 and quickly wrote an antislavery article that was published on March 8, 1775, in the *Pennsylvania Journal and the Weekly Advertiser*. A few weeks later an antislavery society was formed in Philadelphia, with Paine as a founding member. His article started with a clear condemnation of slavery and the Americans who supported it:

> That some desperate wretches should be willing to steal and enslave men by violence and murder for gain, is rather lamentable than strange. But that many civilized, nay, Christianized people should approve, and be concerned in the savage practice, is surprising; and still persist, though it has been so often proved contrary to the light of nature, to every principle of Justice and Humanity, and even good pol-

icy, by a succession of eminent men, and several late publications.[38]

Certainly Jefferson was familiar with Paine and the arguments against slavery. Certainly Jefferson was aware of the existence of the idea that all humans had an equal claim to liberty
and the argument that Africans should be considered human in
these matters. Certainly there were many different ideas about
the institution of slavery and racism in play at the time. So, we
are not judging Jefferson by the standards of our time when we
point out the way in which racism was employed to justify the
barbarism of slavery. We are acknowledging that others in
Jefferson's time—including such notable figures as Paine—
articulated antislavery and antiracist principles, at the same
time that Jefferson was in 1781 writing in his "Notes on the State
of Virginia"[39] about the natural inferiority of blacks.

In that work, Jefferson explained that skin color is crucial,
which led him to conclude, "Are not the fine mixtures of red and
white, the expressions of every passion by greater or less suffusions of colour in the one, preferable to that eternal monotony,
which reigns in the countenances, that immoveable veil of black
which covers all the emotions of the other race?" Smell was an
issue for Jefferson as well. Blacks "secrete less by the kidnies, and
more by the glands of the skin, which gives them a very strong
and disagreeable odour," he explained. Among his other
"insights" into Africans:

---

[38] http://www.thomaspaine.org/Archives/afri.html.
[39] http://etext.lib.virginia.edu/toc/modeng/public/JefVirg.html.

• "They seem to require less sleep. A black, after hard labour through the day, will be induced by the slightest amusements to sit up till midnight, or later, though knowing he must be out with the first dawn of the morning."

• "They are at least as brave, and more adventuresome. But this may perhaps proceed from a want of forethought, which prevents their seeing a danger till it be present. When present, they do not go through it with more coolness or steadiness than the whites."

• "Comparing them by their faculties of memory, reason, and imagination, it appears to me, that in memory they are equal to the whites; in reason much inferior, as I think one could scarcely be found capable of tracing and comprehending the investigations of Euclid; and that in imagination they are dull, tasteless, and anomalous."

And then there is the question of sex. Jefferson believed in the "superior beauty" of whites, noting "the preference of the Oranootan [orangutan] for the black women over those of his own species." He also observed that black men "are more ardent after their female: but love seems with them to be more an eager desire, than a tender delicate mixture of sentiment and sensation." It is unclear whether when Jefferson raped his slave Sally Hemings he was trying to provide a little tenderness in her life that black partners apparently could not. Nor is it clear whether Jefferson spent much time wondering whether his preference for a black woman meant he had something in common with the Oranootan.

Wait just a minute—Jefferson raped a slave? The author of the Declaration of Independence was not only a slave-owner but a rapist?

That description is not heresy but simple logic.[40] The historical consensus is that Jefferson had sex with Sally Hemings, one of the 150 slaves at Monticello, the Jefferson plantation. Even the official guardian of the Jefferson legacy acknowledges this: "The DNA study, combined with multiple strands of currently available documentary and statistical evidence, indicates a high probability that Thomas Jefferson fathered Eston Hemings, and that he most likely was the father of all six of Sally Hemings's children appearing in Jefferson's records."[41]

Rape is defined as sex without consent. Slaves do not consent to their enslavement. To ask whether a slave consents to any particular order given by a master under such conditions is a meaningless question. Sally Hemings was a slave. Thomas Jefferson owned her. Jefferson had sex with Hemings. Therefore, Jefferson raped Hemings, who under conditions of enslavement could not give meaningful consent. That he raped her at least once we know with "high probability." That he raped her five other times is "most likely." That he raped her numerous other times is certainly plausible.

This is hardly surprising; white slave owners routinely raped their slaves. When stated generically—"white masters sometimes raped their African slaves"—the statement doesn't spark controversy. What reason is there to assume Jefferson was different? Since he was willing to own other human beings and force them to work, why would we expect him to be unwilling

---

[40] For further analysis, see Andrea Dworkin, "Race, Sex, and Speech in Amerika," in *Life and Death* (New York: Free Press, 1997), pp. 179–195.

[41] Thomas Jefferson Foundation, which owns and operates Monticello. http://www.monticello.org/plantation/hemingscontro/dnareport6.html.

to force at least one of them to have sex? Why should the same term applied to other slave owners not be used to describe Jefferson's conduct? Yet Americans seem to have a strong need to tell a different story about Jefferson, even when acknowledging these unpleasant realities about his life. Take, for example, the way that liberal television journalist Bill Moyers described the interaction between master and slave as he discussed "the contradiction at the heart of the American experience":

> The hands of Thomas Jefferson that wrote, "life, liberty and the pursuit of happiness," also stroked the breasts and caressed the thighs of a slave woman named Sally Hemings, who bore him six children and whom he never acknowledged.[42]

Although it is true that Jefferson didn't acknowledge those six children, a more pertinent fact for Hemings's children likely was that Jefferson owned them upon their birth. It also is not clear how Moyers knew that Jefferson "stroked" and "caressed" Hemings, given that rapists typically do not concern themselves with the emotions of their victims. It is possible, of course, that he developed feelings for her that were manifested in some degree of tenderness and that the tenderness was reciprocated. Without more extensive evidence, it's difficult to know. What we do know is that Moyers's choice of language elides the reality of the relationship between slave owner and slave, turning rape into lovemaking.

I know of no history textbook in which there is an acknowledgment that Jefferson raped at least one of his slaves. Why?

---

[42] Bill Moyers interview with Sissela Bok, *NOW with Bill Moyers*, July 2, 2004. http://www.pbs.org/now/transcript/transcript327_full.html.

Because to acknowledge such things that bluntly is to take a step on the road to coming to terms with the three racist holocausts that have formed the United States of America. It's to acknowledge that the story we tell ourselves about this country is as much myth as fact. It's to face the ugly, brutal, violent racist history of the country; understand that our affluent society is the product of that history; and then recognize that such violence continues to protect our affluence and perpetuate racialized disparities in the worldwide distribution of wealth.

History matters. It matters whether we tell the truth about what happened centuries ago, and it matters whether we tell the truth about more recent history. It matters because if we can't, we will never be able to face the present, guaranteeing that our future will be doomed. That isn't meant hyperbolically: I mean doomed. I mean that a society with such inequality at so many levels is unsustainable. Martin Luther King Jr. spoke to the sense of urgency in this struggle the night before he was assassinated. On April 3, 1968, in Memphis, he warned that "if something isn't done, and in a hurry, to bring the colored peoples of the world out of their long years of poverty, their long years of hurt and neglect, the whole world is doomed."[43]

There is no way to chart a path forward to avoid that fate without being honest about facts of our past. We also must be honest about the emotions of the present.

---

[43] Martin Luther King Jr., "I See the Promised Land," in *A Testament of Hope: The Essential Writings and Speeches of Martin Luther King, Jr.*, James M. Washington, ed. (New York: HarperCollins, 1991), p. 280.

THE EMOTIONS OF WHITE SUPREMACY:
GUILT, FEAR, AND ANGER

THE PRIMARY FORCE that keeps white supremacy firmly in place is the material and psychological gains that come to white people, which are bolstered by an ideological support system. Over the past two centuries there have been countless attempts—in religion and philosophy, in the various sciences and pseudosciences—to justify white supremacy through rational argument. But the more crucial support for white supremacy is emotional, not rational. White people not only have to prosper under the system, but they have to somehow believe in the system. In the end, I think emotion is more important than reason in this realm.

Some of these emotions come under the general heading of hubris and arrogance—a kind of irrational self-confidence based on being white in a white-supremacist society. When one looks around and sees white people running the show, it's easy to understand why many white people would get the idea that being white makes one special. But the emotions of white supremacy are more complex than that. It is easy to see how arrogance serves to keep white people from critical self-reflection, but more important is to understand how these other emotions—most notably guilt and fear—also help keep white supremacy in place.

Guilt

James Baldwin wrote, "No curtain under heaven is heavier than that curtain of guilt and lies behind which white Americans hide."[44] That curtain remains as heavy today as when he published that in 1965. Unfortunately, most white Americans' guilt ends up dead-ended because it remains unexamined, which contributes to the resiliency of white supremacy. The task is to separate sadness from guilt and then develop an understanding of when a sense of guilt is appropriate.

White people often say they feel guilty about slavery or about racism more generally. In that sense, guilt is irrational and counterproductive. When I think about slavery, I do not feel guilty. I feel sad—incredibly sad—just as I do when I think about the many manifestations of greed and cruelty through the ages. We humans are capable of incredible barbarism, and it's not surprising that those barbaric acts can spark in us sadness, empathy, and compassion for the victims. Part of what it means to be human in the social sense is the capacity for those emotions; without them, social life is impossible. That sense of sadness about slavery is, of course, not limited to white people. Everyone can—and the overwhelming majority of people do—feel it. White people have no special claim to sadness because it was some of our ancestors who maintained the system.

---

[44] James Baldwin, *Collected Essays* (New York: Library of America, 1998), p. 725. This essay, "The White Man's Guilt," was first published in *Ebony* in 1965.

Guilt over slavery, however, is nonsensical. Guilt implies responsibility, and I cannot be responsible for something that existed before I was born. Much the same can be said of racism as a system. It predates my birth and is maintained by forces that I cannot change by action on my own. I don't feel guilty about the existence of racism as a historical system. So why is such guilt so common among white people? I think many white people stay stuck in that sense of guilt about being white for two reasons. First, if one keeps the focus on that abstract sense of guilt, one rarely gets to the appropriate guilt for specific racist actions; it's a convenient way to avoid accountability. Second, such guilt is a way for white people to avoid taking action. If one feels guilty, it is easy to feel paralyzed, which makes it easy not to act. A white person can say, "Look how guilty I feel about racism and white privilege. I feel so bad it immobilizes me." From that position, just talking about race and racism becomes too overwhelming, and people often use their own psychological angst to escape political responsibility.

There are, however, more productive ways to understand white guilt. There are things about which I can, and should, feel guilty. Again, guilt implies responsibility. And I am responsible for two things in this realm: (1) those racist acts that I have committed in my life, and (2) my failures to do all that I can to resist white supremacy and contribute to changing a racist system.

The first category is clear. If I were to discriminate against someone based on race or tell a racist joke, I should feel guilty. When we do things that are unfair, immoral, and harmful to others, guilt is an appropriate emotional response. In fact, it's a necessary part of the process of coming to terms with ourselves and changing our behavior. We all can think of situations in our lives where we did something wrong—failed to keep a promise, betrayed a friend, lied to protect ourselves from the consequences of a mistake—and felt guilty. And we can see that the guilt was the right thing to feel, and (one hopes) spurred us to repair the damage if possible and not repeat the mistake.

In this arena, I can recall a particularly painful incident from my past. In one of my jobs as a journalist I was responsible for the final copy editing for a few regional sections of a newspaper. That meant I worked with several other copy editors who each had primary responsibility for one of those sections. Most of us were in our twenties, some right out of college. All these editing jobs required riding herd on a large number of details under deadline conditions, which meant it could be stressful, especially for new employees who were learning the system. Into that setting one day came a new editor, whom I'll call Jane. She was like the rest of us except that she was black in a newsroom that was overwhelmingly white. At the time, the late 1980s, the backlash against affirmative action was firmly in place. One heard white people talking all the time about how non-whites who weren't qualified were getting jobs. I usually didn't talk that way, but sometimes I felt that way.

As she learned the system, Jane had a few rough nights, as did everyone else. It was a pretty friendly desk, and usually when people had a bad night others would pitch in to help, taking a break from their own tasks to try to make sure a colleague made deadline. People sometimes complained when others were not as productive or efficient as they could be, but in general we all got along. The difference in Jane's case was the talk by some (including me) about how she must be an affirmative-action hire and couldn't really seem to do the job. Did some of us reach that conclusion because she really was failing to make the grade? Or was she just going through the normal adjustment period like most people, only that we were more grudging in our help? At the time, I remember thinking I was being rigorously fair because I thought I was holding Jane to consistent standards. I remember talking to our supervisor to inform her that Jane was not cutting it. I remember being quite proud of myself for, as I saw it, being willing to be blunt and honest.

Shortly after this period, I moved on to graduate school. Jane continued working there before moving to another newspaper. I didn't give her, or those evenings on the desk, much thought until some years later, after I had started studying race and racism and was involved in trying to defend affirmative action on my campus. I started thinking about Jane, and I started to re-evaluate my behavior. After years of not thinking about it, I had to face a painful reality: In dealing with Jane on the desk, I had been a real jerk. I had been a racist jerk. Instead of asking, as I would have if she had been white, "How can I help a new employee learn her job and fit in?" I immediately asked, "What is wrong with this person and why did she get hired?" In other words, before I had any reason to think Jane wasn't up to the job, I made assumptions, and those assumptions affected the way I treated her, actually making it more difficult for her to do the job.

When I realized that, I felt guilty, and it's a good thing that I did. The guilt I felt at that moment came from the recognition that I had done something wrong and possibly hurt someone else. Guilt was an appropriate response. From that guilt, I could think about what had happened and try to avoid repeating the behavior in the future. The guilt, the awareness of a mistake, was part of the process of moral and political self-evaluation. I couldn't go back and change what I had done, but I could make sure I didn't do it again.

In some sense, that kind of guilt is easy to deal with. There is a clear action that one can identify, try to understand, and come to terms with. If possible, one can take steps to try to rectify any damage done to others. The second kind of guilt that I should feel—the guilt over not working hard enough to change a white-supremacist society—is more complicated and disturbing. In a general sense, we all have a responsibility to make our society a better place. That responsibility certainly varies depending on one's power and privilege; those of us with the resources—time, money, education, experience, opportunities—to contribute to progressive social change bear a share of that burden consistent with our resources. And those of us who benefit, by choice or not, from the inequities in the system carry an extra responsibility.

I am white and male, educated and trained in research and writing, materially comfortable in a stable job with status that gives me considerable control over how I use my time. In a white-supremacist society, I clearly have obligations that can't be ignored. I have tried to work toward racial justice. Have I done enough? Certainly not. I can look at my personal, professional, and political lives and see places where I could do more, where others have done more. Does that mean I think I am some kind of superman who believes he can do everything and fix every problem? No, but it does mean that if I am honest, I can always see that there are opportunities to push myself. That's why being honest can be so hard. That state of affairs—recognizing I haven't done enough and could do more—is never going away, if I'm honest about myself and the world in which I live. I could glibly say that recognition of that fact doesn't bother me, but it does, fairly often. I don't obsess about it, but I am aware of it, and it leads to a variety of emotions — sadness, anger, resolve, and sometimes guilt. Here the guilt is trickier, because if I let myself sink too far into that guilt, I will reduce my political effectiveness. It's tempting to repress that sense of guilt completely or wallow in it; both reactions are born out of a frustration with the complexity of the world and a desire to simplify the moral equation. But our task is to live on the edge of the guilt, to use it to challenge ourselves and each other to do better.

The balance in all this is tricky. It's easy to become self-absorbed, to spend too much time reliving one's own life and mistakes. At the same time, the tendency among whites toward self-congratulation, denial, and avoidance is widely known, especially to non-white people. For example, early in my teaching career my department's predominantly white faculty met to discuss problems around race and ethnicity. Although everyone was willing to acknowledge that we live in a racist society and that we all carried some of that racism in us, there seemed to be more explanations for why other people might have problems than there was honest introspection.

At that point in the semester, I had just had an African-American student who had been having problems in class, and I had come to realize too late that my failure to reach out to help her may have had something to do with my unexamined assumptions about race. When I have a white student who is performing poorly, I tend to see a failing student. But I realized that I had been thinking of this student as a failing *black* student.

Was I unconsciously working off of racist stereotypes that led me to assume she couldn't do university-level work? I wasn't sure. So, I posed the question to the group: Does anyone else struggle with this problem of seeing race as an explanation for failure, but only with non-white students? How do you deal with it?

The question hung in the air for a moment, dropped on the table, and met a silent death. After some uncomfortable shifting in chairs, the group moved on. No one seemed willing to engage the issue. I tell that story not to appear holier than thou; my failing was real, and it is a problem I struggle with years later, though I think I have made real progress. I raised it in the meeting not to make people uncomfortable but because I was looking for help in dealing with the question. At first, I was confused about why my question had been such a conversation-stopper. I thought that by turning the focus on myself and not indicting anyone else, I could help people feel comfortable with talking about a difficult subject. But later I realized that precisely by making an abstract topic real, by admitting that I was struggling with a very serious manifestation of the society's racism that lived in me, I had threatened my colleagues who did not want to see themselves that way. To give voice to the problem—even if I only talked about myself—was to make it too real, too threatening. The fear in the room at that moment was thick. It is important to talk about that fear.

Fear

It seems slightly self-indulgent to talk about the fears of white people in a white-supremacist society. After all, what do white people really have to be afraid of in a world structured on white privilege? It may be self-indulgent, but it's critical to understand because these fears are part of what keeps many white people from confronting ourselves and the system.

The first, and perhaps most crucial, fear is the fear of facing the fact that some of what we white people have is unearned. It's a truism that we don't really make it on our own; we all have plenty of help to achieve whatever we achieve. That means that some of what we have is the product of the work of others, distributed unevenly across society, over which we may have little or no control individually. No matter how hard we work or how smart we are, we all know—when we are honest with ourselves—that we did not get where we are by merit alone. And many white people are afraid of that fact.

A second fear is more crass: White people's fear of losing what we have—literally the fear of losing things we own if at some point the economic, political, and social systems in which we live become more just and equitable. That fear is not completely irrational; if white privilege—along with the other kinds of privilege many of us have living in the middle class and above in an imperialist country that dominates much of the rest of the world—were to evaporate, the distribution of resources in the United States and in the world would change, and that would be a good thing. We would have less. That redistribution of wealth would be fairer and more just.[45] But in a world in which people have become used to affluence and material comfort, that possibility can be scary.

A third fear involves a slightly different scenario—a world in

---

[45] For further discussion, see Robert Jensen, "What Is a Moral Level of Consumption?" *Counterpunch*, October 30, 2003. http://www.counterpunch.org/jensen10302003.html.

which non-white people might someday gain the kind of power over whites that whites have long monopolized. One hears this constantly in the conversation about immigration, the lingering fear that somehow "they" (meaning not just Mexican Americans and Latinos more generally, but any non-white immigrants) are going to keep moving to this country and at some point become the majority demographically. Even though whites likely can maintain a disproportionate share of wealth, those numbers will eventually translate into political, economic, and cultural power.[46] And then what? Many whites fear that the result won't be a system that is more just, but a system in which white people become the minority and could be treated as whites have long treated non-whites. This is perhaps the deepest fear that lives in the heart of whiteness. It is not really a fear of non-white people. It's a fear of the depravity that lives in our own hearts: Are non-white people capable of doing to us the barbaric things we have done to them?

A final fear has probably always haunted white people but has become more powerful since the society has formally rejected overt racism: The fear of being seen, and seen through, by non-white people. Virtually every white person I know, including white people fighting for racial justice and including myself, carries some level of racism in our minds and hearts and bodies. In our heads, we can pretend to eliminate it, but most of us know it is there. And because we are all supposed to be appro-

---

[46] For a particularly blunt expression of this view by a white establishment intellectual, see Samuel P. Huntington, "The Hispanic Challenge," *Foreign Policy*, March/April 2004. http://www.foreignpolicy.com/story/cms.php?story_id=2495.

priately antiracist, we carry that lingering racism with a new kind of fear: What if non-white people look at us and can see it? What if they can see through us? What if they can look past our antiracist vocabulary and sense that we still don't really know how to treat them as equals? What if they know about us what we don't dare know about ourselves? What if they can see what we can't even voice?

I work in a large university with a stated commitment to racial justice. All of my faculty colleagues, even the most reactionary, have a stated commitment to racial justice. And yet the fear is palpable. An example:

A Chicana student came to my office once after leaving another class, where a discussion had started about the language of race. A white student had tried to derail a serious conversation by joking, "I don't know what I'm supposed to call you people. Hispanic? Mexican American?" The Chicana student got frustrated and angry as the white student kept joking about it, ignoring the political implications of the question. I knew the professor in the class, a white person. I asked the student how the professor had handled it. She said the professor said nothing, leaving her to cope with the white student alone. The discussion in class apparently ended with everyone frustrated and confused. The Chicana student was still angry when she came to my office, not only with the white guy in class but also with the professor, for not helping her deal with it. Why didn't the professor say something?

I can't know for sure, but here's my guess: The white professor saw unfolding before her a tense situation. Given her responsibilities in the class, the professor should have at some point intervened, not to try to eliminate the tension, but to guide the discussion so that something productive could result from the tension. That likely would have meant pointing out to the white student (and to the whole class) that his comments were trivializing a serious issue, and asking the student (and the whole class) to consider how we sometimes use such diversionary tactics to avoid serious discussion of racial issues. That's easy to say, when one is making a judgment from the outside and after the fact. Those tense scenes often emerge quickly, forcing us to make decisions quickly about how to respond. Still, that's what professors get paid for, and we have a duty to deal with it—especially those professors who say they want to engage such topics in the classroom. Instead, this professor in this moment stepped back and failed to meet her responsibilities, letting the students flounder. A teachable moment was lost. The whole class lost out, and the Chicana student was forced to bear the burden of the white student's racial hostility. The professor failed.[47]

Why would a professor who has a commitment to social justice pass up a chance to educate and let a non-white student struggle alone like that? Again, I can't know for sure, but here's my guess: The professor was afraid. Afraid not just of the tenseness and volatility of the situation, but also afraid of stepping into the fray and possibly making a mistake. What if she said the wrong thing? What if in saying the wrong thing she revealed that she carried in her some lingering traces of racism? What if she

---

[47] Looking back, I should note here that I failed, too. Once I heard this story, I had a responsibility to engage with my colleague. I did not, partly out of recognition that a history of conflict with this particular person would have made it difficult, but likely also out of a desire to avoid a potentially unpleasant situation.

said something that allowed the non-white students in class to see her? To see through her?

It is a fear I have struggled with, and I remember the first time I ever articulated that fear in public. I was on a panel with several other professors at the University of Texas discussing race and politics in the O. J. Simpson case. Next to me was an African-American professor. I was talking about media; he was talking about the culture's treatment of the sexuality of black men. As we talked, I paid attention to what was happening in me as I sat next to him. I felt uneasy. I had no reason to be uncomfortable around him, but I wasn't completely comfortable. During the question-and-answer period — I don't remember what question sparked my comment — I turned to him and said something like, "It's important to talk about what really goes on between black and white people in this country. For instance, why am I feeling afraid of you? I know I have no reason to be afraid, but I am. Why is that?"

My reaction wasn't a crude physical fear, not some remnant of being taught that black men are dangerous (though I have had such reactions to black men on the street in certain circumstances). Instead, I think it was that fear of being seen through by non-white people, especially when we are talking about race. In that particular moment, for a white academic on an O. J. panel, my fear was of being exposed as a fraud or some kind of closet racist. Even if I thought I knew what I was talking about and was being appropriately antiracist in my analysis, I was afraid that some lingering trace of racism would show through, and that my black colleague would identify it for all in the room to see. After I publicly recognized the fear, I think I started to let go of some of it. Like anything, it's a struggle. I can see ways in which I have made progress. I can see that in many situations I speak more freely and honestly as I let go of the fear. I make mistakes, but as I become less terrified of making mistakes I find that I can trust my instincts more and be more open to critique when my instincts are wrong.

I feel guilty every day, and that's appropriate. I feel afraid every day, and that's understandable. The important question: What am I willing to do? To help us move forward on that, we need to get angry.

Anger

Here's what I think white people need emotionally: Less fear, less abstract guilt, more anger.

Less fear of ourselves and more risk-taking. Less guilt about things we didn't do or can't change and more action about the things we did and can change. More righteous anger. Not self-righteousness, but righteous anger rooted in a commitment to justice, the kind of anger that helps us shed our fears and let go of our unproductive guilt. The kind of anger that can help us find our place and our voice in social movements seeking justice. The kind of anger that comes from desperation when we realize how powerful an oppressive system is, how deep are the injuries it causes, how destructive it is to everyone's lives including the privileged. The older I get, the angrier I get. People keep telling me that I need to mellow out, find a way to deal with my anger. I have a way to deal with it: I let it out, strategically (I hope). An example:

At a symposium on journalism ethics I attended several years ago, the keynote speaker was a well-known white journalist who talked about journalists' special role in society as guardians of democracy. Because of that, journalists are sometimes allowed to do certain things that other citizens are not, such as intrude into people's private lives. This is much like doctors who are allowed to cut into people or soldiers who are allowed to kill, he said.

Then he offered another analogy: It's like police, he said, who "have the right to beat people."

I sat in the audience, momentarily stunned. I nudged a friend next to me. Had he actually said that, that police have a right to beat people? I looked around at an almost completely white and generally middle-class audience in the auditorium of the private college where the symposium was being held. No one seemed too upset by what he had said. I was. I was angry.

The speaker went on to say several other things with which I disagreed. Later, during the question period, I went to the microphone, intending to focus on another point he had made. "But before I get to my question," I said, "I want to say that it seems to me that anyone who can say that police have a right to beat people is presumptively excluded from a discussion about ethics of any kind." The audience squirmed, unsure of how to react. The speaker winced but never responded to my challenge in public. During the reception that followed his talk, he made a beeline over to me to argue. He was upset not so much because I had challenged him but because I had made it clear that I thought his response to my other question was insufficient, and I wouldn't concede that he had defended his position adequately. I continued to think he was wrong. The exchange ended without a resolution of the issue.

As I stood there taking stock of that exchange, another member of the audience told me she was unclear what point I was trying to make. Surely the speaker just misspoke, she said. What the speaker must have meant to say was that in certain situations, police have the legal right to use force, sometimes even deadly force. Yes, I understood that, I replied. But my point was that he used the phrase "the right to beat people." The language reflects his relationship to power. No one who comes from a class of people subject to being beaten by police would ever think of using such a phrase. Only people who don't have to worry about being beaten would make the "mistake." Unless they insert themselves into certain kinds of political struggles, white, professional, middle-class people generally don't worry a lot about being beaten by police. Beyond that, I argued, it's plausible that the speaker and lots of other folk like him are glad they live in a world in which police sometimes beat people; it keeps the "dangerous classes" in line.

This person shrugged and said I was overreacting to an admittedly careless, but harmless, choice of words on the speaker's part. She turned, apparently never really understanding what I thought was a simple point, and headed off to talk to someone less contentious.

Then another member of the audience came up to me and suggested that I should have curbed my anger in asking my question, pointing out that I hadn't persuaded the speaker of my points. "You catch more flies with honey than vinegar," he said, smug and self-satisfied. I disagreed, arguing that my anger had been appropriate. My goal in speaking was not to persuade the speaker; frankly, I had no reason to think (based on what I knew about him) that he was willing to listen. My anger was directed at him, but my main message was for the audience, I said. I was communicating to them that what the speaker had said was unacceptable, and that anger was the appropriate response. Being soft-spoken, I said, would have sent the wrong message; I should have been mad—everyone should have been mad. He repeated his assertion that being gentler would have been more effective, without offering any response to my point, and walked away, as self-satisfied as when he initially approached me.

At that point, I was really angry, not so much at the speaker but at everyone else in the room. I was angry at all the nice middle-class white people who were too polite to say anything, to hold the speaker accountable. I was especially angry at the three or four white people who had come up to me after the talk and thanked me for speaking up. I bit my tongue and didn't ask them the obvious question: Why didn't you speak up, too, instead of leaving my comments to hang in the air, to wither and die without support? Looking back, it was a mistake to bite my tongue with them. I should have told them I was angry with them, too.

A lot more anger in that room at that moment would have made for a much more productive event.

Roots of the anger

We live in a morally lazy society, which should make us angry. I do not mean morally lazy in the same sense that traditionalists and fundamentalists condemn contemporary America. The problem is not a decline in family values (whatever those may be), but the ease with which people who could intervene on the side of justice—primarily the white middle class—not only don't but refuse to acknowledge the scope of the problems and their own connection to them. How does one persuade an affluent and protected class of people to work for fundamental change in regard to an issue such as race? And how does one make people see the connection between the racism that lives at home with the racism in U.S. policies abroad that are so brutal, both economically and militarily?

Some of the great thinkers about race, especially W. E. B. DuBois, saw this connection clearly. As a socialist and an anti-imperialist, as well as a critic of race relations in the United States, DuBois could see clearly the country's seamless history of oppression. I invoke DuBois not just because of the keenness of his insights or eloquence of his writing, but for quite strategic purposes. The connections I want to make among white supremacy, our economic system, and the actions of the U.S. government in world affairs are often dismissed these days with arrogant talk of the inevitability of markets, the naturalness of capitalism, the grand victory of the West in the cold war, and the inherent goodness of the United States in the so-called war on terrorism. If he were alive, DuBois would surely scoff at such self-indulgent triumphalism. As he put it in "The Souls of White Folk," an essay written after World War I as the United States was making claim to being the world's exemplar:

> It is curious to see America, the United States, looking on herself, first, as a sort of natural peacemaker, then as a moral protagonist in this terrible time. No nation is less fitted for this role. For two or more centuries America has marched proudly in the van of human hatred. . . . Instead of standing as a great example of the success of democracy and the possibility of human brotherhood America has taken her place as an awful example of its pitfalls and failures, so far as black and brown and yellow peoples are concerned.[48]

---

[48] W. E. B. DuBois, *Darkwater: Voices from Within the Veil* (Mineola, N.Y.: Dover, 1999), p. 28.

Nothing that has happened since DuBois wrote would change his fundamental analysis. The United States continues to pursue an economic and military policy abroad that offers as its underlying assumption a simple but quite bizarre assertion: The primary beneficiaries of the resources, both human and natural, of developing countries—that is, the countries of the "black and brown and yellow peoples" of the world—should not be those people but corporations and wealthy investors in the United States. Should it be a surprise that a country founded on genocide and slavery moved on to consolidate its power and wealth through the subjugation or destruction of non-white peoples elsewhere? DuBois certainly would not be surprised. Nor should we be.

If we care about racial justice—as well as justice on other issues—we should be, individually and collectively, moved to oppose both the government that carries out these policies and the economic structures in which they are rooted. Yet, for the most part, the class that has the time, energy, and money to be effective politically—the white middle class, the class to which I belong—remains passively complicit in, or actively supportive of, these policies. All this makes me angry, at others and at myself for not being more politically effective.

Struggling to get beyond the anger

Why do so many people choose not to act? Why do people take steps to make sure they don't know about injustice? How am I to deal with the anger at that inaction and my growing sense of alienation from the people most like me? A friend, who isn't white, is not optimistic about those questions. "The problem with most Americans is that they have no soul," he told me. He uses the term soul in a political, not a theological sense. He means that people so comfortable materially can easily lose sight of anything other than the maintenance of that level of comfort. Without even thinking about it, they trade their souls for affluence.

I am more upbeat than he is, not necessarily because I analyze the situation differently, but because I have no choice. To believe in the possibility that the white middle class in the United States can change is, in essence, to assert a belief in myself, and in the possibility that I will not drown in this anger. That especially matters to me because the anger never stays in me as anger; it almost always turns to a deep sadness. I can live with the anger; I can manage it and find ways to vent it in the company of allies and friends. But the sadness is less controllable; it simply sits in me. Putting that sadness into words so it can be vented is more difficult, sometimes impossible.

So, I have no choice but to try to get beyond the anger, lest I be consumed by it and trapped forever in the sadness. Anger can, and should, be deployed strategically. But if not controlled, it makes conversation, and hence politics, impossible. That means I have to find ways to talk with people whom I might otherwise want to separate myself from. In short, I have come to realize that my political work as a middle-class white man in the United States is primarily with the white middle class. But that work is always more than simply providing information or analysis. More important is breaking through the willed ignorance, the purposeful not-knowing about the racialized consequences of our social, political, and economic structures and policies—the not-knowing that makes possible the comfortable lives we of that race and class lead. The task is to give people who otherwise need not care about justice a reason to care.

That means those of us who are white and want to be part of movements to change these systems and structures of power have to rein in our instincts to feel self-righteous and understand that in every human interaction there is the potential for connection and transcendence. We have to find the space between the surface triumphalism of our times proclaimed by politicians and pundits, and the deeper cynicism that many ordinary people feel. We have to get angry, stay angry, but not let that anger swallow us. We have to let our passion for justice fuel our work but also make sure it doesn't lead us to overlook our own flaws and failures.

This takes a deep capacity to live in humility, something privileged people get too little practice in. Some are better at holding onto that humility than others. I try, but I fail all too often.

PLAYING THE FOOL

T HE RECENT PERSONAL failure that shook me the most happened in the spring of 2004 when I stepped onto the speak-
ers' platform at the Virginia Festival of Books in Charlottesville
with *Newsday* editor Les Payne to discuss our chapters in the
book *When Race Becomes Real*,[49] edited by Bernestine Singley,
the other panelist. As I walked to my seat, I was well aware of
Payne's impressive record. I had read his work, and I knew he
was a more experienced journalist who had won more prizes
and written more important stories than I. Payne had traveled
more widely and reported on more complex subjects. He was
older and had done more in his life than I had. I also had heard
Payne speak before and knew that he was a more forceful and
commanding speaker.

So, as I sat down at my seat, I did what came naturally: I felt
superior to him. If it seems odd that I would feel superior to
someone older and more experienced, whom I knew to be more

---

[49] Bernestine Singley, ed., *When Race Becomes Real: Black and White
Writers Confront Their Personal Histories* (Chicago: Lawrence Hill
Books, 2002).

talented and accomplished than I am, here is another relevant fact: Les Payne is black.

I didn't recognize that feeling of superiority as I sat down, or as I made my remarks on the panel. It wasn't until Payne started reading from his chapter and explaining how he came to write his essay that my feeling became so painfully clear to me. Payne talked about how, as a teenager born in the segregated South who attended high school in the North, he had struggled to overcome the internalized sense of inferiority which grew from the environment in which he had been raised. He talked with a quiet passion and power, about how deeply that sense of inherent inferiority can take root in African Americans.

At some point in his talk, I made the obvious connection. Part of the reason that the struggle Payne described is so hard for African Americans is because white people are so often expressing, through their behavior as well as words, a feeling of superiority. My mind raced immediately to that feeling of superiority that I felt as we had taken our seats. I had assumed— despite all that I knew about Payne, his record, and his speaking ability—that I would be the highlight of the panel. Why? It might be because I was a particularly egotistical white boy. Maybe I was a white boy with delusions of grandeur. The former is almost certainly true. The latter, I hope, is at least a slight exaggeration. But whatever my personal weakness, one factor is obvious: I am white and Payne is black, and that feeling of superiority was rooted in that fact.

The moment that particular understanding hit me, I was literally left speechless, fighting back tears and a profound sense of despair. I struggled to keep focused on Payne's words, but it was difficult as I tried to cope with what I was feeling. Payne finished, and Singley started her reading. Later, when the discussion period began, I did my best to answer a question asked of me, but I remained shaken.

Why all of this drama? Because I'm supposed to be one of the "good" white people, one of the antiracist white people. I am politically active, and have worked hard to incorporate an honest account of race and racism into my teaching, writing, political work, and life. But in that moment, I had to confront the fact that a basic psychological feature of racism was still very much part of me. As Payne talked honestly of struggling with a sense of inferiority, I had to face that I had never really shaken a sense of my superiority. On the platform with Payne that day, his words forced me to feel it. That wasn't his intention; he was speaking to the primarily African-American audience, not to me. Whatever his intent, however, he did me that service. But I am most grateful to Payne not for that, but for something that happened later. After the event, I was planning to drive to Washington, D.C. When I mentioned that to Payne, he asked if he could ride with me and catch a flight from D.C. back to New York. I jumped at the chance, in part because I wanted to hear more about the research for the book on Malcolm X he was writing, but also because I wanted to talk to him about what had happened to me on stage.

In the few hours we drove together, I took advantage of Payne's experience in journalism and asked his opinion about a range of issues, in addition to pumping him for insights into Malcolm X's life. And, finally, I asked if I could tell him about what had happened on stage. It turned out, not surprisingly, that Les Payne is a gracious man. He listened to my story, nodding throughout. Nothing I said seemed to shock him. He is, after all, black in the United States; I didn't expect that I would shock him. It was after I had finished that Payne did something for which I will always be grateful: He didn't forgive me. He made no attempt to make me feel better. He didn't reassure me that I was, in fact, one of the good white people. He simply acknowledged what I had told him, said he understood, and continued our discussion about the politics of race in the United States.

Part of me probably wanted him to forgive me. Part of me probably wanted the approval of a black person at that moment, to help eliminate the discomfort, which I was still feeling. But what would that have accomplished for him, for me, or for the world? Without knowing it, Payne during the panel had given me the gift of feeling uncomfortable, of forcing me to face myself. In the car, perhaps with full knowledge of what he was doing, he gave me the gift of not letting me off the hook.

When I dropped him at the airport, I had no illusions. The day had meant much more to me than to him. He had been willing to teach me something, and then he went on to other things. His personal struggle with internalized inferiority was over; his chapter in the book made that clear, as did his interaction with me. It was easy to tell by the way he spoke and carried himself that Payne doesn't spend a lot of time worrying about whether white people are better than he. But I was left with the unfinished project of dealing with my internalized sense of superiority. And it was clear to both of us that such a project was my responsibility, not his.

The story of that day in Charlottesville can't end there, of course. On the platform with us was Bernestine Singley, who is every bit as black as Les Payne, and is an accomplished lawyer, writer, and speaker. Why am I focusing on him and not her?

Why did he spark this realization in me and not her? In part it was because of what Payne talked about on stage; his remarks and his chapter had pushed my buttons. Also, I have known Singley longer and have a more established relationship with her. I consider her (and I hope she considers me) a trustworthy ally and comrade in the struggle. Singley and I also have very different styles, and when we appear on panels together we clearly are not competing.

With all that said, it's also difficult to miss the fact that Singley is a woman and Payne is a man. There was not only a race dynamic on stage, but a gender dynamic. It's likely that I was, in classic male fashion, focusing on the struggle for dominance with the other man on the panel. This perception of myself also is hard to face; in addition to being a good white person, you see, I'm also one of the "good" men. I'm one of the men on the correct side in gender politics. But I also am one of the men who, whatever side he is on, constantly struggles with the reality of living in a male-supremacist society that has taught me lessons about how to vie for dominance. Introspection on these matters is difficult; people in privileged positions often are not in the best position to evaluate our own behavior. But looking back on that day, it appears to me I walked onto that platform with an assumption of my inherent superiority—so deeply woven into me that I could not in the moment see it—that had something to do with race and gender. Those assumptions make it hard to reach a conclusion other than: I was a fool.

I use that term consciously, because throughout history white people have often cast non-whites, especially blacks, as the fool to shore up our sense of superiority. But in that game, it is white people who are the fools, and it is difficult and painful to confront that. We have to face the ways in which white supremacy makes white people foolish and forces others to pay a price for our foolishness.

I propose that we white people admit that we are mostly all fools within a white-supremacist society. It's crucial that we be able to laugh at ourselves. By that I don't mean laugh about the issue; there is nothing funny about white supremacy, and the struggle for racial justice is not a joke. But we are often fools. I propose we try that, instead of racing to either figure out which white people are racists and which are nonracist, or simply declaring all white people racist. What if we just acknowledged that? I am often a fool. I am a white person living in a white-supremacist society who still sometimes feels racist feelings in his body, thinks racist thoughts in his head, and acts in subtle (and on occasion, not-so-subtle) racist ways in the world. I struggle. I try to correct my mistakes. I try to find ways to be accountable. I don't want to be congratulated for it. I'm not looking for absolution.

I would say I am an antiracist person who often succeeds at resisting the embedded racism of the culture, when I can see it. Even though I sometimes fail, I am different than a colleague who really believes that black people are intellectually inferior—and we all know there are white people who hold such views, even if it is no longer polite to speak them in public. That difference makes a difference in the world, especially if it leads us white people not just to applaud ourselves for personal strides but to work in solidarity with others on the larger and more difficult questions of institutionalized racism.

My point is that white people who struggle against racism need not deny what they have achieved. In fact, it is by acknowledging those achievements that we open up the space to go further, both individually and collectively, in resisting the society's racism and one day eliminating it. It doesn't mean we are off the hook; it means we are on the hook even more publicly.

How public should we be about our foolishness?

When I published a version of this account of my experience with Les Payne on the Internet, I got a variety of responses, including some angry ones from black people. One correspondent put it bluntly: How dare I feel superior to Les Payne? There was outrage in her e-mail, which I understood. The notion that I could even consider the idea that I would be superior to such a person angered her, and she condemned me for it. There is no way for me to argue with such an assessment; I could hardly criticize her for articulating the truth.

But it raised a recurring, and difficult, question for me that others had raised in the past: How honest should white people be in public—in mixed-race settings where non-white people can listen in—about the arrogance and pathology of whiteness? I wrote that account out of the hope that it could help white people deal with a feeling that I think many of us struggle with but is difficult to acknowledge because it is so depraved. But is that appropriate in public?

I have long wrestled with a similar question in regard to feminist work on sexual violence and the sex industry. The way men talk about women and sex in all-male spaces is often brutal and cruel. The pornography produced in the United States often reflects that brutality and cruelty. Men have to come to terms with how our sexual imaginations are formed, how we are socialized to accept such inhumanity and find pleasure in it. But is it fair to talk about that in public? Don't women have enough to cope with, without forcing them to confront the pathology of men in such blunt form?

I struggle with this question and have no simple answer. It is true, of course, that no pathology can be confronted if it remains in the shadows, if we don't find a way to make it visible. But if non-white people and women already bear a considerable burden because of the actions of white people and men, are there limits to what should be aired in public? There's a cliché in antiracist circles that sometimes white people have to come together alone to work out these things, without imposing on non-white people. That's true enough and can be done in some settings. But the nature of mass media means that once something is put out in public, it can't be contained to whites-only spaces. And even if it could, is there a value for everyone in such honesty?

This is not a question on which a white person can simply poll non-white people to determine what to do. Opinions, in all communities, will vary. Obviously, by virtue of my writing this, I have decided that the potential value outweighs the potential harm. I reached that decision after talking to many people, non-white and white. But in the end it was my decision, for which I am accountable. Whether in the final accounting it turns out that I made the right decision, it's a reminder of the reality of privilege. No matter how hard it was for me to confront my foolishness and pathology, I don't experience the most costly burdens of white supremacy.

Given white people's ability, at least in the short term, to escape those burdens, it is tempting simply to try to opt out, to avoid some of the more difficult confrontations with self and others. When we recognize that a serious commitment to resisting racism means facing these difficult questions, and also facing the fact that it's almost certain that we will at times act foolishly and fail, it's easy to turn away. In fact, it's easy to blame those who continue to raise the issues, as if they are responsible for perpetuating the problem, as if white supremacy and privilege would disappear if we simply ignored it. One often hears the question: "Do you have to politicize everything?"

The answer, of course, is yes.

AGAINST DIVERSITY, FOR POLITICS

"A GAINST DIVERSITY" MAY seem like an odd phrase in a book that critiques white supremacy. So, let me be clear: I am not against a diverse world in which diverse peoples and cultures are valued and supported. But I am against diversity as a substitute for politics.

In this world there is a diversity of species, which makes possible life as we know it and is the source of much joy, beauty, and mystery. In the human species there is a diversity of persons and cultures, both of which also are the source of joy, beauty, and mystery. Diversity is a fact of our existence, and vital to what makes human life engaging and meaningful. I do not want to thwart the fostering of diversity by individuals or institutions. I do not want to suppress the many differences that exist between racial, ethnic, cultural, or sexual groups. Nor do I want members of dominant groups to ignore or denigrate those differences. I do not want a single culture to pave over cultural differences. Unfortunately, in many times and places in this country diversity has been, and sometimes still is, suppressed, often quite brutally. We should be grateful for the social, political, and cultural changes that have made it easier for people to live in their diversity, while at the same time remembering that in some places people continue to be punished—psychologically, physically, economically, socially—not so much for being "diverse" but, more accurately, for being diverse and refusing to subordinate themselves to a dominant culture. We have much work to do to maintain and extend the space in which diversity can flourish here.

I'm all for diversity and its institutional manifestation, multiculturalism. But we should be concerned about the way in which talk of diversity and multiculturalism has proceeded. After more than a decade of university teaching and political work, it is clear to me that a certain kind of diversity-talk actually can impede our understanding of oppression by encouraging us to focus on the cultural and individual, rather than on the political and structural.

Instead of focusing on diversity, we should focus on power. The fundamental frame for pursuing analyses of issues around race, ethnicity, gender, sexuality, and class should be not cultural but political, not individual but structural. Instead of talking about diversity in race, class, gender, and sexual orientation, we should critique white supremacy, economic inequality in capitalism, patriarchy, and heterosexism. We should talk about systems and structures of power, about ideologies of domination and subordination—and about the injuries done to those in subordinate groups, and the benefits and privileges that accrue to those in dominant groups.

Here's an example of what I mean: A professor colleague, a middle-aged heterosexual white man, once told me that he thought his contribution to the world—his way of aiding progressive causes around diversity issues—came by expanding his own understanding of difference and then working to be the best person he could be. He said he felt no obligation to get involved in the larger world outside his world of family and friends, work and church. In the worlds in which he found himself, personal and professional, he said he tried to be kind and caring to all, working to understand and celebrate difference and diversity.

There are two obvious problems with his formulation, one concerning him as an individual and one concerning the larger world. First, without a connection to a political struggle, it is difficult for anyone to grow morally and politically. My own experience has taught me that it is when I am engaged in political activity with people across identity lines that I learn the most. It is in those spaces and those relationships that my own hidden prejudices and unexamined fears emerge, in situations in which comrades whom I trust can hold me accountable. Without that kind of engagement, I rarely get to levels of honesty with people that can propel me forward.

The colleague in question saw himself as being, as the cliché goes, a sensitive new age guy, but from other sources I know that he continued to behave in sexist ways in the classroom. Because he had no connection to a feminist movement—or any other liberatory movement where women might observe his behavior and be in a position to hold him accountable—there was no systematic way for him to correct his sexist habits. His self-image as a liberated man was possible only because he made sure he wasn't in spaces where women could easily challenge him.

The second problem is that if everyone with privilege—especially the levels of privilege this man had—decided that all they were obligated to do in the world was to be nice to the people around them and celebrate diversity, it is difficult to imagine progressive social change ever taking place. Yes, we all must change at the micro level, in our personal relationships, if the struggle for justice is to move forward. But struggle in the personal arena is not enough; it is a necessary but not sufficient criterion for change. Lots of white people could make significant progress toward eliminating all vestiges of racism in our own psyches—which would be a good thing—without it having any tangible effect on the systems and structures of power in which white supremacy is manifested. It would not change the ways in which we benefit from being white in that system. It doesn't mean we shouldn't "work on" ourselves, only that working on ourselves is not enough.

It is possible to not be racist (in the individual sense of not perpetrating overtly racist acts) and yet at the same time fail to be antiracist (in the political sense of resisting a racist system). Being not-racist is not enough. To be a fully moral person, one must find some way to be antiracist as well. Because white people benefit from living in a white-supremacist society, there is an added obligation for us to struggle against the injustice of that system.

The same argument holds in other realms as well. Men can be successful at not being sexist (in the sense of treating women as equals and refraining from sexist behaviors) but fail at being antisexist if we do nothing to acknowledge the misogynistic system in which we live and try to intervene where possible to change that system. The same can be said about straight people who are relatively free of antigay prejudice but do nothing to challenge heterosexism, or about economically privileged people who do nothing to confront the injustice of the economic system, or about U.S. citizens who don't seek to exploit people from other places but do nothing to confront the violence of the U.S. empire abroad.

We need a political and structural, rather than a cultural and individual, framework. Of course we should not ignore differences in cultural practices, and individuals should work to change themselves. But celebrating cultural differences and focusing on one's own behavior are inadequate to the task in front of us. I have been clearer on that since September 11, 2001, after which George W. Bush kept repeating "Islam is a religion of peace," reminding Americans that as we march off on wars of domination we should respect the religion of the people we are killing. Across the United States after 9/11, people were saying, "I have to learn more about Islam." My response was, "Yes, but you also have to learn more about American foreign policy and militarism." Religious and cultural differences can be extremely important in understanding political struggles, but those differences do not by themselves explain politics. Too many non-Muslim Americans were too quick to believe that they could understand the U.S. attacks on Afghanistan and Iraq by reading a book about Islam.

It is an improvement when an insular people become curious about something outside their own experience. But when politicians can so easily invoke diversity and multiculturalism in the service of the empire, something has gone dangerously off the rails. It is strange enough when an antifeminist administration can make the claim that its invasion of Afghanistan was motivated in part by a feminist desire to free the women of that country, but even stranger when some segments of the feminist movement celebrated the invasion and, hence, participated in the celebration of militarism. When feminism can be a cover for a war of empire, we're in trouble.

Let me return to the title of his chapter and, once again, make sure I am clear about its meaning.

I grew up in North Dakota, a very homogeneous world—very white, very middle class, very insular. Since then I have been lucky to live in more diverse places, where I have made friends who don't look exactly like me. I have learned, and continue to learn, a lot about other people and other cultures. I continue to learn not to make the assumption that everyone else sees the world as I do, or wants the same things I do, or interprets my words and actions the same way I do. These are lessons I was glad to learn, and struggle to relearn almost daily. Diversity is a good thing, and learning how to deal with diversity is a good thing, too. The project of helping people achieve what is sometimes called "cultural competence"—especially those of us who provide services to a diverse population, such as teachers or health-care workers—is important. But diversity training and cultural competence, while valuable in their own right for their own purposes, are not the same thing as political resistance to unjust systems and structures of power. Diversity and cultural awareness are necessary to progressive social change but not sufficient to achieve it. If we allow diversity to become the mantra for issues around white supremacy and white privilege, we are in for trouble.

One of the things I fear most about using diversity as the framework is how easy it is for some of the less pleasant truths about this society and its affluence to drop out of our conversations. Diversity is fine, so long as it doesn't seriously challenge the desires of the dominant society. Diversity is fine, so long as the distribution of power and wealth remains relatively constant. Diversity is fine, so long as it stays in a cultural box.

How do we dismantle white supremacy?

So, if it's about politics not culture, it's reasonable to expect something beyond vague exhortations and be more specific about what kind of politics I'm talking about. What is my plan? What are my solutions?

I will resist the temptation to offer a list of actions needed, not only because I don't feel qualified to proclaim them but also because solutions are always contextual; they depend on the specific problems we face in the world in a given time and place. There is no easy template for putting together a successful program for changing unjust policies or systems. From the past we can reasonably observe that all successful movements for justice include public education and organizing—helping people develop an analysis and then creating channels for action based on that analysis. Beyond that, there are specific lessons from specific movements that can be applied to specific situations, but to talk generally about what people should be doing is difficult.

I have no blueprint for people to follow and no priority list of issues we white people should commit to. We live in a society in crisis on multiple fronts—political, economic, cultural, and ecological. There's no shortage of issues for those concerned with racial justice, and justice more broadly, to take up. Some of those struggles are aimed directly at white supremacy, such as campaigns against racism in law enforcement and the police brutality that follows from that racism.[50] Some in the black

---

[50] For example, the Texas Criminal Justice Coalition works on these issues around the state. http://www.criminaljusticecoalition.org/.

community have taken up the project of reparations for the descendants of African slaves.[51] There are organizations engaged in such work; anyone can join them.[52]

Beyond those kinds of activities, in any social justice movement there are ways white people can challenge white supremacy. Members of environmental organizations can press to make sure that issues of environmental racism—the way in which poor communities that typically are non-white so often become dumping grounds for toxic waste—are on the agenda for their group. Labor organizers can work to make sure that unions, many of which have a racist history, are open in meaningful ways to non-white workers. People concerned with the state of public education can put high on their groups' list of priorities the struggle to equalize resources for all students and end de facto educational apartheid.

So, there are times when white people can find a place in organizations run by non-white people, fitting ourselves into the agendas that they have set. We can lend our energies and resources to the campaigns of others. We can leverage our privileges and resources to the benefit of such projects. We also can make sure racial-justice politics are on the agenda in predominantly white groups. We can seek ways to connect across racial lines in a society that for many of us is still largely segregated in housing and social patterns. We can look for ways in the all-white settings many of us find ourselves in to keep race visible, knowing that in such settings it is easy to forget. The choices

---

[51] See Randall Robinson, *The Debt: What America Owes to Blacks* (New York: Dutton, 2000).

[52] http://www.reparationscentral.com/links1.html.

about where and how to use our energies and resources are always complex.

For example, at various times I have participated in efforts to defend affirmative action, not because I think affirmative action is the solution to the problem of white supremacy at the University of Texas or in the United States, but because it was an issue on which many non-white people had decided to focus, it opened a space in which one could talk about racism, and there was a way for me to contribute as a member of the university community. As events in the world have unfolded since 9/11, my focus increasingly has shifted to the complexity of race in antiwar and antiempire activism, which always has an anti-racist component given the way in which U.S. wars and economic policies target and disadvantage non-white people around the world. I also have for a number of years worked in the feminist antipornography movement, which includes an analysis not only of the misogyny of mass-marketed pornography but also the blatant white supremacy of some pornographic genres that draw on ugly racist stereotypes.

If I were to attempt any statement about solutions, it is that progressive social change requires one to go forward with passion and a sense of commitment in what one is fighting for, while at the same time being realistic about just how much one really understands a complex world. Those two things often are in conflict. To find the courage and energy it takes to stand against power, one has to believe deeply in the cause. There are few traditional rewards of status or material wealth to be gained in movements for progressive social change, and the more radical the movement, the fewer the rewards. So, the motivation for most people is passion and a belief that we are right. But at the same time, we have to retain an understanding that while we may be right in some sense about the quest for justice, our specific analysis at any given moment may be slightly off, or maybe even drastically wrong. If we are not open to influences that can help us see that, if we do not hold onto intellectual and moral humility, we are more likely to make mistakes, possibly quite serious mistakes, at some point. This is especially true of people in the more privileged sectors of society. This is especially true of white people in the United States. It certainly has been true in my life.

One general principle can help guide us in these endeavors: As we struggle with how to confront these systems of power and privilege, we should go toward that which most frightens us. This is especially true for us white people trying to work against white supremacy. When we are dealing with issues of oppression, we are most likely to make progress when we face the things that we wish we did not have to face. In the words of the late poet and activist Audre Lorde, who wrote so clearly and fiercely about both the barriers that difference creates and the possibility of transcending those differences: "I urge each one of us here to reach down into that deep place of knowledge inside herself and touch that terror and loathing of any difference that lives there. See whose face it wears."[53]

The moments when I have gotten close to touching that terror are both frightening and exhilarating. They wash me clean and, at the same time, leave permanent scars. I sometimes rush toward those moments and other times do not have the strength to get

---

[53] Audre Lorde, "The Master's Tools Will Never Dismantle the Master's House," in *Sister Outsider* (Freedom, Calif.: Crossing Press, 1984), p. 113.

too close. I am afraid of failing, of being seen and seen-through. I remain terrified, and yet I continue to seek out that terror as often as I can bear it, for one simple reason: Those are the moments in my life when I come closest to tasting real freedom.

CONCLUSION
White People's Burden

T HE UNITED STATES is a white country. By that I don't just mean that the majority of its citizens are white, though they are (again, for now but not forever). What makes the United States white is not the fact that most Americans are white but the assumption—especially by people with power—that American equals white. Those people don't say it outright. It comes out in subtle ways. Or, sometimes, in ways not so subtle.

Here's an example: I'm in line at a store, unavoidably eavesdropping on two white men in front of me, as one tells the other about a construction job he was on. He says: "There was this guy and three Mexicans standing next to the truck." From other things he said, it was clear that "this guy" was Anglo, white, American. It also was clear from the conversation that this man had not spoken to the "three Mexicans" and had no way of knowing whether they were Mexicans or U.S. citizens of Mexican heritage. It didn't matter. The "guy" was the default setting for American: Anglo, white. The "three Mexicans" were not Anglo, not white, and therefore not American. It wasn't "four guys standing by a truck." It was "a guy and three

Mexicans." The race and/or ethnicity of the four men were irrel-
evant to the story he was telling. But the storyteller had to mark
it. It was important that "the guy" not be confused with "the
three Mexicans."

Here's another example, from the Rose Garden. At a 2004
news conference outside the White House, President George W.
Bush explained that he believed democracy would come to Iraq
over time:

> There's a lot of people in the world who don't believe that
> people whose skin color may not be the same as ours can be
> free and self-govern. I reject that. I reject that strongly. I
> believe that people who practice the Muslim faith can self-
> govern. I believe that people whose skins aren't necessar-
> ily—are a different color than white can self-govern.[54]

It appears the president intended the phrase "people whose
skin color may not be the same as ours" to mean people who are
not from the United States. That skin color he refers to that is
"ours," he makes it clear, is white. Those people not from the
United States are "a different color than white." So, white is the
skin color of the United States. That means those whose skin is
not white but are citizens of the United States are . . . ? What are
they? Are they members in good standing in the nation, even if
"their skin color may not be the same as ours"?

This is not simply making fun of a president who sometimes
mangles the English language. This time he didn't misspeak, and
there's nothing funny about it. He did seem to get confused when
he moved from talking about skin color to religion (Does he

---

[54] George W. Bush, remarks at White House, April 30, 2004. http://www.
whitehouse.gov/news/releases/2004/04/20040430-2.html

think there are no white Muslims?), but it seems clear that he intended to say that brown people — Iraqis, Arabs, Muslims, people from the Middle East, whatever the category in his mind — can govern themselves, even though they don't look like us. And "us" is clearly white. In making this magnanimous proclamation of faith in the capacities of people in other parts of the world, in proclaiming his belief in their ability to govern themselves, he made one thing clear: The United States is white. Or, more specifically, being a real "American" is being white. So, what do we do with citizens of the United States who aren't white?

That's the question for which this country has never quite found an answer: What do white "Americans" do with those who share the country but aren't white? What do we do with peoples we once tried to exterminate? People we once enslaved? People we imported for labor and used like animals to build railroads? People we still systematically exploit as low-wage labor? All those people — indigenous, African, Asian, Latino — can obtain the legal rights of citizenship. That's a significant political achievement in some respects, and that popular movements that forced the powerful to give people those rights give us the most inspiring stories in U.S. history. The degree to which many white people in one generation dramatically shifted their worldview to see people they once considered to be subhuman as political equals is not trivial, no matter how deep the problems of white supremacy we still live with. In many comparable societies, problems of racism are as ugly, if not uglier, than in the United States. If you doubt that, ask a Turk what it is like to live in Germany, an Algerian what it's like to live in France, a black person what it's like to live in Japan. We can acknowledge the gains made in the United States — always understanding those gains came because non-white people, with some white allies, forced society to change—while still acknowledging the severity of the problem that remains.

But it doesn't answer the question: What do white "Americans" do with those who share the country but aren't white?

We can pretend that we have reached "the end of racism" and continue to ignore the question. But that's just plain stupid. We can acknowledge that racism still exists and celebrate diversity, but avoid the political, economic, and social consequences of white supremacy. But, frankly, that's just as stupid. The fact is that most of the white population of the United States has never really known what to do with those who aren't white. Let me suggest a different approach.

Let's go back to the question that W. E. B. DuBois said he knew was on the minds of white people. In the opening of his 1903 classic, *The Souls of Black Folk,* DuBois wrote that the real question whites wanted to ask him, but were afraid to, was: "How does it feel to be a problem?"[55] DuBois was identifying a burden that blacks carried—being seen by the dominant society not as people but as a problem people, as a people who posed a problem for the rest of society. DuBois was right to identify "the color line" as the problem of the twentieth century. Now, in the twenty-first century, it is time for whites to self-consciously reverse the direction of that question at heart of color. It's time for white people to fully acknowledge that in the racial arena, we are the problem. We have to ask ourselves: How does it feel to be the problem?

---

55 W. E. B. DuBois, *The Souls of Black Folk* (New York: Vintage, 1990), p. 7.

That is the new White People's Burden, to understand that we are the problem, come to terms with what that really means, and act based on that understanding. Our burden is to do something that doesn't seem to come naturally to people in positions of unearned power and privilege: Look in the mirror honestly and concede that we live in an unjust society and have no right to some of what we have. We should not affirm ourselves. We should negate our whiteness. Strip ourselves of the illusion that we are special because we are white. Steel ourselves so that we can walk in the world fully conscious and try to see what is usually invisible to us white people. We should learn to ask ourselves, "How does it feel to be the problem?"

So, the question isn't what should be done about those in the United States who aren't white, but what should be done about those who are white. Maybe we should all be shipped back to Europe where we (or our ancestors) came from. Maybe we should be subject to a little tough love—no more unearned benefits from society until we clean up our act. Or maybe we should start by openly telling the truth: Whiteness—the whole constellation of practices, beliefs, attitudes, emotions that are mixed up with being white—is the problem. Whiteness is degraded and depraved, an insane belief that one can find meaning in life simply by virtue of being on top of a racial hierarchy. To the degree that we accept any of the meaning that the dominant society gives to whiteness, we white people are degraded and depraved. To the degree those illusions of superiority linger in me, I am degraded and depraved.

Don't confuse this book with some feel-good, self-help project. When I face these things about myself and about the world in which I live, I usually don't feel better. As I have already said, it makes me incredibly sad. Such feelings are inevitable; if we take seriously the project of racial justice, how could we not be sad? There is a process we white people have to go through, and it isn't always fun. It starts with recognizing the reality of white supremacy, which should lead us toward serious attempts to change our own lives and join with others to change society. To makes those changes possible, we have to go through a process that will be painful if it is undertaken seriously. If we are serious about asking ourselves what it feels like to be the problem, it will hurt. That hurt will be nothing like what non-white people endure because of white supremacy, but if white people struggle to be fully human there is a cost. If we let ourselves see and feel the human costs of white supremacy, can we expect to be happy all the time?

This is the only way out of the trap. If any white person wants to take seriously an honest struggle with whiteness, it doesn't lead directly to some land of love and harmony. In my experience, it is a long, difficult road. Walking that road is painful, with no guarantees about the rewards at the end. All we know is that there are rewards along the way, as one gains a better sense of one's own humanity. We should consider James Baldwin's observation in 1962: "White Americans know very little about pleasure because they are so afraid of pain."[56] Baldwin is one of the best commentators I have read on the experience of being white. In a 1965 essay he pointed out that blacks learn to live with racism, but whites remain deformed by it:

> [W]hat happens to the poor white man's, the poor white woman's mind? It is this: they have been raised to believe,

---

56 James Baldwin, *Collected Essays* (New York: Library of America, 1998), p. 677. This essay "Color" was first published in *Esquire* in 1962.

and by now they helplessly believe, that no matter how terrible some of their lives may be and no matter what disaster overtakes them, there is one consolation like a heavenly revelation—at least they are not black. I suggest that of all the terrible things that could happen to a human being that is one of the worst. I suggest that what has happened to the white Southerner is in some ways much worse than what has happened to the Negroes there.[57]

Later that same year he wrote more about white people's struggles, pointing out how white people's fear of an honest dialogue confronting racism also constrains black people's freedom to speak:

Moreover, the history of white people has led them to a fearful, baffling place where they have begun to lose touch with reality—to lose touch, that is, with themselves—and where they certainly are not truly happy, for they know they are not truly safe. They do not know how this came about; they do not dare examine how this came about. On the other hand, they can scarcely dare to open a dialogue which must, if it is honest, become a personal confession—a cry for help and healing, which is, really, I think, the basis of all dialogues—and, on the other hand, the black man can scarcely dare to open a dialogue which must, if it is honest, become a personal confession which, fatally, contains an accusation. And yet, if neither of us cannot do this, each of us will perish in those traps in which we have been struggling for so long.[58]

---

[57] Ibid., p. 716. This essay, "The American Dream and the American Negro," was first published in the *New York Times Magazine* in 1965.

[58] Ibid., p. 724–725. This essay, "The White Man's Guilt," was first published in *Ebony* in 1965.

If we white people can fashion a personal confession in which we ask ourselves how it feels to be a problem, then perhaps we can face the accusations that will come our way in the personal confessions of non-white people. For white people, that is our task, our burden. Our "White People's Burden."

The old version of the "White Man's Burden" was a call to bring civilization to the darker people of the world. The first lines of Rudyard Kipling's poem set the tone for his ode to empire, to the false nobility of white supremacy:

> Take up the White Man's burden—
> Send forth the best ye breed—
> Go bind your sons to exile
> To serve your captives' need.

We long have known that what the "captives" need is to be spared the alleged generosity and benevolent tutelage of white people. The "captives" of white supremacy do not need the best that we white people breed; they don't need our sons to run their lives. What they need from white people is for us to realize we are the problem. They need us to commit to dismantling white supremacy as an ideology and a lived reality.

The world does not need white people to civilize others. The real White People's Burden is to civilize ourselves.

RECOMMENDED READINGS
ON RACE AND ETHNICITY

Baldwin, James. *Collected Essays* (New York: Library of America, 1998).

Black Commentator. http://blackcommentator.com/.

Crow Dog, Mary. *Lakota Woman* (New York: Grove, 1990).

Deloria Jr., Vine. *Custer Died for Your Sins: An Indian Manifesto* (Norman: University of Oklahoma Press, 1988).

DuBois, W. E. B. *The Souls of Black Folk* (New York: Vintage, 1990/1903).

Dyson, Michael Eric. *I May Not Get There with You: The True Martin Luther King Jr.* (New York: Free Press, 2000).

Feagin, Joe R. *Racist America: Roots, Current Realities, and Future Reparations* (New York: Routledge, 2000).

Gonzalez, Juan. *Harvest of Empire: A History of Latinos in America* (New York: Penguin, 2000).

Kelley, Robin D. G. *Yo' Mama's Disfunktional: Fighting the Culture Wars in Urban America* (Boston: Beacon, 1997).

Kivel, Paul. *Uprooting Racism* (Philadelphia: New Society Publishers, 1996).

Lipsitz, George. *The Possessive Investment in Whiteness* (Philadelphia: Temple University Press, 1998).

Lorde, Audre. *Sister Outsider* (Freedom, Calif.: Crossing Press, 1984).

Malcolm X. *Malcolm X Speaks: Selected Speeches and Statements,* George Breitman, ed. (New York: Grove, 1965).

Newkirk, Pamela. *Within the Veil: Black Journalists, White America* (New York: New York University Press, 2000).

Omi, Michael, and Howard Winant. *Racial Formation in the United States: From the 1960s to the 1990s,* 2nd ed. (New York: Routledge, 1994).

Roediger, David R., ed. *Black on White: Black Writers on What It Means to Be White* (New York: Schocken, 1998).

Singley, Bernestine, ed. *When Race Becomes Real: Black and White Writers Confront Their Personal Histories* (Chicago: Lawrence Hill Books, 2002).

Takaki, Ronald. *Strangers from a Different Shore: A History of Asian Americans* (New York: Little Brown and Co., 1989).

Williams, Patricia. *The Alchemy of Race and Rights* (Cambridge: Harvard University Press, 1991).

Wise, Tim. *White Like Me: Reflections on Race from a Privileged Son* (New York: Soft Skull Press, 2005).

ABOUT THE AUTHOR

Robert Jensen is an associate professor of journalism at the University of Texas at Austin, where he has taught courses on media law, ethics, and politics since 1992. He is the author of *Citizens of the Empire: The Struggle to Claim our Humanity* (City Lights, 2004); *Writing Dissent: Taking Radical Ideas from the Margins to the Mainstream* (Peter Lang, 2001); co-author with Gail Dines and Ann Russo of *Pornography: The Production and Consumption of Inequality* (Routledge, 1998); and co-editor with David S. Allen of *Freeing the First Amendment: Critical Perspectives on Freedom of Expression* (New York University Press, 1995). Jensen is a founding member of the Nowar Collective (http://www.nowarcollective.com) and a member of the board of the Third Coast Activist Resource Center (http://thirdcoastactivist.org). He also writes for popular media, and his opinion and analytic pieces on foreign policy, politics, and race have appeared in *USA Today*, *Los Angeles Times*, *Philadelphia Inquirer*, *Newsday*, *Houston Chronicle*, *Dallas Morning News*, *Atlanta Journal-Constitution*, *The Hindu* (India), *Al-Ahram* (Cairo), *The Progressive*, and on web sites including Alternet, Common Dreams, Counterpunch, and ZNet.